PRACTICE BOOK

·3·
WORLD OF LANGUAGE

SILVER BURDETT GINN

PARSIPPANY, NJ • NEEDHAM, MA

Atlanta, GA • Irving, TX • Santa Clara, CA • Deerfield, IL

Contents

◆ UNIT 7 ◆

◆ UNIT 8 ◆

Writing Sentences

> A **sentence** is a group of words that tells a complete thought.

A. Circle the group of words in each pair that is a sentence.
The first one is done for you.

1. (Amelia Earhart loved planes.)

   Was a famous pilot.

2. First to fly alone from Hawaii to California.

   She broke many flying records.

3. Tried to fly around the world alone.

   Her plane vanished in 1937

4. Earhart was never found.

   Will always be remembered.

5. Won an award for courage.

   She wrote a book about flying.

B. Match a group of words from each column below to make a sentence.

6. Many people	brings jet fuel to the plane.
7. A tank truck	check seat belts.
8. The jet engines	board the jetliner.
9. The captain	begin to roar.
10. Flight attendants	zooms into the sky.
11. The big airplane	welcomes the passengers.

WRITE IT

Write about what you might see from an airplane. Be sure each of your sentences tells a complete thought. Write on a separate sheet of paper.

Writing Sentences

The groups of words below are not sentences.

Ray throws the.
Hits the ball.

Write your own words to complete each thought.
Use the picture to help you.

1. Ray throws the _____ .

2. _____ hits the ball.

 A **sentence** is a group of words that tells a complete thought. When a group of words does not tell a complete thought, it is not a sentence.

A. Circle each group of words that is a sentence. The first one is done for you.

1. (The Aces are a baseball team.)

2. The player is ready to hit the ball.

3. The first strike.

4. She hit a home run.

5. High in the sky and into the crowd.

6. The Aces won the game.

7. On the field with the coach.

8. Swings the bat.

B. Write each sentence you circled.

EXAMPLE: _The Aces are a baseball team._____

9. _____

10. _____

11. _____

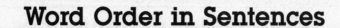

Word Order in Sentences

 The words in a sentence must be in an order that makes sense.

A. Underline the group of words that does not make sense. Write a sentence that makes sense by changing the order of the words.

1. Plants need water. need also sunshine They.

   _____

2. Roots under ground grow the. Most stems grow upward.

   _____

3. water Roots carry stems to. They also hold a plant in place.

   _____

4. tubes Stems tiny have. The tubes bring food to plants.

   _____

B. Two words in each sentence are in the wrong order. Underline them. Then write the sentence correctly.

5. Trees grow on tall plums.

   _____

6. He waters the day every plant.

   _____

WRITE IT

Write about a plant you have seen. Make sure the words in your sentences are in order and make sense. Write on a separate sheet of paper.

Word Order in Sentences

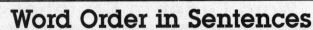

Fill in the box next to the word group that makes sense.

☐ **1.** Stories are wonderful his.
☐ **2.** His stories are wonderful.

Sentence **1** does not make sense. The words are not in the right order. Did you fill in the box next to sentence **2**? The words are in an order that makes sense.

⟶ The words in a sentence must be in an order that makes sense. Changing the order of words sometimes changes the meaning of a sentence.

A. Underline the groups of words that make sense. The first one is done for you.

1. <u>Samuel Clemens was a writer.</u> **3.** He Missouri lived in.

2. Clemens was born in 1835. **4.** His home was by a river.

B. Write the words in an order that makes sense.
EXAMPLE: Clemens characters created funny.
Clemens created funny characters. _____

5. used He the name Mark Twain.

_____

6. He about wrote Tom Sawyer.

_____

C. Write new sentences. Change the order of the underlined words. The first one is done for you.

7. <u>Clemens</u> wrote about <u>people</u>. People wrote about Clemens. ___

8. Tom traveled <u>up</u> and <u>down</u> the river.

_____

Statements and Questions

The first word of a sentence begins with a **capital letter.** A **statement** is a sentence that tells something. It ends with a period (.). A **question** is a sentence that asks something. It ends with a question mark (?).

A. Read each sentence below. Circle the end mark. Then write <u>statement</u> or <u>question</u> next to each.

1. How do dogs help people? _____

2. Dogs herd cattle and sheep. _____

3. They pull heavy sleds through snow. _____

4. What else can dogs do? _____

5. The first animal in space was a dog. _____

B. Follow the girl until she finds her dog. Circle any small letters that should be capital letters. Fill in each blank with a period or a question mark.

WRITE IT

Write questions about dogs. Then write statements that answer the questions. Write on a separate sheet of paper.

Statements and Questions

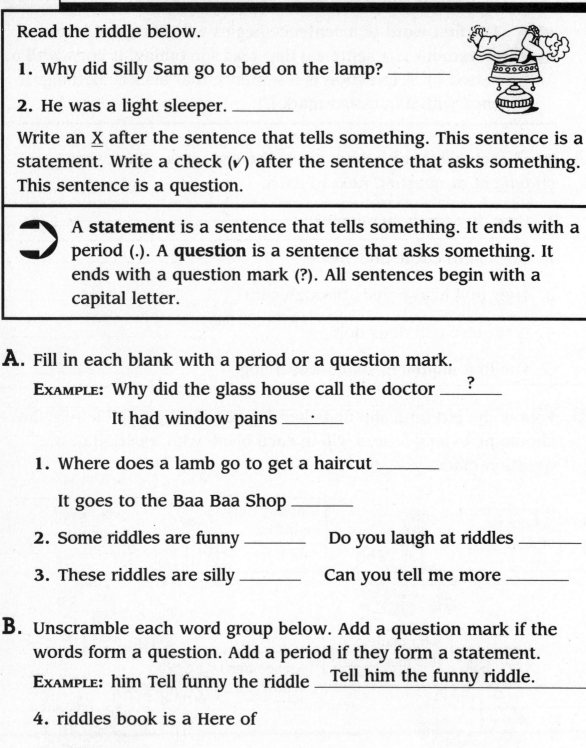

Read the riddle below.

1. Why did Silly Sam go to bed on the lamp? _____

2. He was a light sleeper. _____

Write an X after the sentence that tells something. This sentence is a statement. Write a check (✓) after the sentence that asks something. This sentence is a question.

⟳ A **statement** is a sentence that tells something. It ends with a period (.). A **question** is a sentence that asks something. It ends with a question mark (?). All sentences begin with a capital letter.

A. Fill in each blank with a period or a question mark.

EXAMPLE: Why did the glass house call the doctor _____?_____

It had window pains _____·_____

1. Where does a lamb go to get a haircut _____

It goes to the Baa Baa Shop _____

2. Some riddles are funny _____   Do you laugh at riddles _____

3. These riddles are silly _____   Can you tell me more _____

B. Unscramble each word group below. Add a question mark if the words form a question. Add a period if they form a statement.

EXAMPLE: him Tell funny the riddle _Tell him the funny riddle._

4. riddles book is a Here of

_____

5. Do riddles you new like

_____

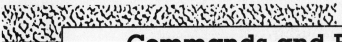

Commands and Exclamations

A **command** is a sentence that gives an order. It ends with a period (.). An **exclamation** is a sentence that shows strong feeling. It ends with an exclamation mark (!).

A. Write a period (.) or an exclamation mark (!) after each sentence. Then write <u>command</u> or <u>exclamation</u>.

1. The treasure hunt is today _____ _____

2. I am so excited _____ _____

3. Study the treasure map _____ _____

4. Start at the red brick house _____ _____

B. Write each command and exclamation correctly. Use a capital letter and the correct end mark.

the alligators are so mean

look for the tree with the X

the chest has jewels in it

turn left at the tree

5. _____

6. _____

7. _____

8. _____

WRITE IT

Write sentences about a time when you found something special. Try to include both an exclamation and a command. Write on a separate sheet of paper.

Commands and Exclamations

Write a sentence. Tell the boy in the picture to go get his raincoat. Use a period (.) as the end mark.

1. _____

Write a sentence about wearing a raincoat. Use an exclamation mark (!) to show strong feeling.

2. _____

⟳ A **command** is a sentence that gives an order. It ends with a period (.). An **exclamation** is a sentence that shows strong feeling. It ends with an exclamation mark (!). All sentences begin with a capital letter.

A. Each sentence below is a command or an exclamation. Fill in the blank with a period (.) or an exclamation mark (!).

EXAMPLE: Today is my birthday _____.

1. I'm so happy _____   3. What fun it is _____

2. Bring your sister _____   4. Call me soon _____

B. Circle each exclamation. Write it correctly.

EXAMPLE: open my present first (it is just beautiful)
It is just beautiful!

5. i love this wrapping paper   take off the ribbon

_____

6. that is my favorite book   pass the book around

_____

7. say good-bye to everyone   the party was so much fun

_____

Sentence Parts

> A sentence has two parts. The **subject** names someone or something. The **predicate** tells what the subject is or does.

A. Draw one line under the subject in each sentence. Draw two lines under the predicate.

1. Young people learn about their country from dolls.

2. Old dolls traveled by wagon to the American West.

3. Sailors carve dolls from bone.

4. My favorite doll opens and shuts its eyes.

5. Some workers fix broken dolls.

B. Draw a line to match each subject with a predicate. Then write the complete sentences.

Subjects	Predicates
Buttons	collect interesting dolls
Some adults	play with soft dolls
Young children	is a famous doll
Raggedy Ann	make good eyes for dolls

6. _____

7. _____

8. _____

9. _____

WRITE IT

Write sentences about a doll or toy you own. Be sure each sentence has a subject and a predicate. Write on a separate sheet of paper.

Sentence Parts

Read the sentence. Then write the word that tells who the sentence is about.

Tanya ate an apple.

1. _____ (subject)

Write the words that tell what Tanya did.

2. _____ (predicate)

 A sentence has two parts. The **subject** names someone or something. The **predicate** tells what the subject is or does. The subject and predicate of a sentence must make sense together.

A. Circle <u>subject</u> if the subject is underlined. Circle <u>predicate</u> if the predicate is underlined.

EXAMPLE: <u>John Chapman</u> lived long ago.   (subject) predicate

1. <u>Americans</u> moved west.   subject   predicate

2. Chapman <u>took apple seeds to Ohio.</u>   subject   predicate

3. <u>He</u> planted the seeds near streams.   subject   predicate

4. Many people <u>called him Johnny Appleseed.</u>   subject   predicate

5. The trees <u>grew throughout the Middle West.</u>   subject   predicate

B. Write the subject of each sentence.

EXAMPLE: Johnny wore a pot on his head.   _____Johnny_____

6. The happy girl found the trees.   _____

7. She ate red and green apples.   _____

8. Her brother climbed the tree.   _____

9. He put the apples in his pocket.   _____

Subjects in Sentences

⟩ The **subject** of a sentence names someone or something.

A. Circle the two groups of words that make sense in the sentence. Write one subject to complete each sentence.

1. Wild animals   Grew taller   Many squirrels

   _____ live in fields and forests.

2. Shallow burrows   Dark caves   Live in groups

   _____ can be homes for wild animals.

3. A lion   Buys plant food   A tiger

   _____ is a member of the cat family.

4. Few buffalo   Many rabbits   Build their homes

   _____ roam the prairies.

B. Complete each sentence with subjects from the sign. Use each subject only once.

Mighty elephants   Leopards   A desert camel ☆ A kangaroo

5. _____ carries people across the sand.

6. _____ have dark spots and long tails.

7. _____ curl their trunks when they fight.

8. _____ leaps with its hind legs and tail.

WRITE IT

Write about wild animals that interest you. Try to use different subjects in your sentences. Write on a separate sheet of paper.

Subjects in Sentences

Write the subject of each sentence. Write the words that tell what or who flew over the tree tops.

1. Eagles flew over the tree tops. _____

2. The kite flew over the tree tops. _____

Every sentence has a subject. The **subject** of a sentence names someone or something.

A. Write the subject in each sentence.

EXAMPLE: One western state
Grow apples   <u>One western state</u> is California.

1. Settlers
   Crossed the ocean   _____ were from Spain.

2. Looked for gold
   Many people   _____ explored the area.

3. Steep cliffs
   Drive away   _____ line the coast.

4. Tall trees
   Fell suddenly   _____ fill the forests.

B. The subject is underlined in each sentence. Write a new subject for each sentence. Choose a new subject from the box.

A traveler	Hot deserts	Its parks	Many states

EXAMPLE: <u>Sandy beaches</u> cover parts of the state.   <u>Hot deserts</u>

5. <u>The forests</u> protect wild animals. _____

6. <u>Several beaches</u> are near the ocean. _____

7. <u>My family</u> visited the Grand Caynon. _____

Predicates in Sentences

⟶ The **predicate** of a sentence tells what the subject is or does.

A. Circle the predicate for each subject.

1. The Chinese New Year   is a popular holiday.

a sunny day.

2. Family members   the first five days.

exchange gifts.

3. Little children   a happy time.

watch the special parades.

4. Many dancers   perform in the Lion Dance.

the colorful, sparkling costumes.

B. Complete each sentence. Write a predicate from the flags below. Use each predicate once.

CLOSE FOR THE HOLIDAY   VISIT EACH OTHER.

CONTINUES FOR FIVE DAYS   COOKS SPECIAL FOODS

5. Chinese New Year _____ .

6. Most shops _____ .

7. Every family _____ .

8. People _____ .

WRITE IT

Write about a holiday you celebrate. Add variety to your writing by using different predicates. Write on a separate sheet of paper.

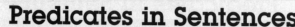

Predicates in Sentences

Look at the picture. Then complete the sentence.
Write what the person is.

1. The person _____ .

Look at the picture again. Complete the sentence.
Write what a firefighter does.

2. A firefighter _____ .

You wrote predicates. You told what the
subject of each sentence is or does.

> Every sentence has a predicate. The **predicate** of a sentence
> tells what the subject is or does.

A. Complete each sentence. Circle the predicates.

EXAMPLE: The children (explored the fire station.)/ a roaring fire.

1. Two girls   sat in the fire truck. / many long days.

2. The truck   near the town hall. / was shiny and clean.

3. The fire alarm   rang loudly. / the hardest job.

4. Some boys   used the fire hoses. / in the class.

B. Complete each sentence. Write a predicate from the box. Use each
predicate only once.

carries hoses and a pump	work together in teams
protect firefighters from smoke	warn of danger

EXAMPLE: Firefighters ___work together in teams___ .

5. A pumper truck _____ .

6. Fire alarms _____ .

7. Gas masks _____ .

Using the Thesaurus

A. Use the following entry from a thesaurus to answer the questions.

bad—not good; not as good as it should be. It was a <u>bad</u> movie, and everyone was bored.

<u>harmful</u>—causing hurt or damage. Buyers were warned that the new toy might be <u>harmful</u>.

<u>naughty</u>—behaving badly; not obeying. The <u>naughty</u> puppy chewed on the table.

<u>poor</u>—not good in quality; without quality. The tennis player made a <u>poor</u> shot and lost the point.

<u>severe</u>—very harsh. Travelers need to be extra careful in <u>severe</u> weather.

<u>wrong</u>—not right. It is <u>wrong</u> to interrupt someone who is speaking.

ANTONYMS: excellent, fine, good, right, superior

1. What is the entry word? _____

2. What is one meaning for <u>bad</u>? _____

3. What is the example sentence for <u>bad</u>? _____

_____

4. How many synonyms are listed for <u>bad</u>? _____

5. Which synonym of <u>bad</u> means "very harsh"? _____

B. Complete each sentence. Write a synonym for <u>bad</u>.

6. Some insects are _____ to plants.

7. The _____ winds knocked down the telephone wires.

8. The team played a _____ game on Saturday.

9. The _____ kitten scratched the chair.

Grade 3, Unit 1
VOCABULARY: Thesaurus (Practice)

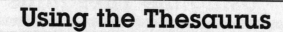

Using the Thesaurus

A **thesaurus** is a book of synonyms, or words that have almost the same meaning. Read the thesaurus entry below. Circle the entry word <u>laugh</u>.

Entry word   **laugh**—to make sounds that show joy or amusement. Do you <u>laugh</u> at elephant jokes?

Synonyms   <u>chuckle</u>—to laugh quietly. They <u>chuckle</u> over funny cartoons.

        <u>giggle</u>—to laugh in a silly or nervous way. Did you <u>giggle</u> when the ride spun you in circles?

        <u>roar</u>—to laugh loudly. You will <u>roar</u> when you see the hilarious show.

        <u>snicker</u>—to make slight or covered laughing sounds in trying not to laugh aloud. Please do not <u>snicker</u> when someone makes a mistake.

Antonyms   ANTONYMS: cry, frown, scowl

A. Write an answer to each question. Use the thesaurus entry above to help you. The first one is done for you.

1. What is the meaning of <u>laugh</u>? <u>to make sounds that show</u>

    <u>joy or amusement</u>

2. What are two synonyms for <u>laugh</u>? _____

3. What is one antonym for <u>laugh</u>? _____

B. Complete each sentence. Write a synonym for <u>laugh</u>.

EXAMPLE: Did she _____ giggle _____ when you found her hiding?

4. They _____ when the bear is surprised.

5. They _____ as six clowns get out of one tiny car.

6. Did you _____ when he gave the wrong answer?

Story Characters and Setting

> **Characters** are the people or animals in a story. **Setting** is when and where the story takes place.

A. Write each character and setting under the correct heading.

the emperor	a tiny hut	evening at the ranch
Peter Pan	near Mount Tam	Dan the Dinosaur

Characters   **Settings**

1. _____   4. _____

2. _____   5. _____

3. _____   6. _____

B. Each sentence tells about a character or a setting. Write <u>character</u> or <u>setting</u> beside each one.

7. Li Po was a shy, lonely boy.   _____

8. The canary often sang songs for him.   _____

9. Li Po's home was small and cozy.   _____

10. One morning the sun was especially   _____
    bright.

11. The long road outside the door   _____
    looked deserted.

12. A small man with a brown sack   _____
    suddenly appeared.

WRITE IT

On a separate sheet of paper, write the name of a character from your favorite story. Write sentences about when and where the story takes place.

Story Characters and Setting

Read the following story beginning. Then answer the questions.

Pam went to Merryville one spring morning. She saw Lily the magician. She wrote a story about Lily for the newspaper.

What two people is this story about? _____ _____

Where does the story take place? _____

When does the story take place? _____

 Characters are the people or animals in a story. **Setting** is the time and place of a story. Every story has characters and a setting.

A. Circle each story character.

EXAMPLE: (Snow White)   near the lake

1. King Arthur   a dark castle
2. last winter   a brave knight
3. Tom Kitten   Grandmother's house
4. a space station   the shoemaker
5. Bambi   late in the afternoon

B. Write the words that are settings on the lines below. The first one is done for you.

6. Rapunzel   10. a summer day in Maine
7. in the park at dusk   11. Winnie the Pooh
8. the land of Oz   12. a clever cat
9. Mr. Appleby   13. Julie's playhouse

    in the park at dusk

_____   _____

_____   _____

A Story Plot

⊃ A **plot** is the series of events in a story. It tells what happens.

A. Write <u>beginning</u>, <u>middle</u>, or <u>ending</u> to tell in which part of the story each event belongs.

1. Anita mixed cream, peanuts, and carrots in a kettle. _____

2. Mother smiled and said, "This soup is filled with love." _____

3. Little Anita wanted to make a special soup for her mother. _____

4. Anita looked through the kitchen for good things to eat. _____

B. Write the sentences above in the correct order to tell a story.

5. _____

_____

6. _____

_____

7. _____

_____

8. _____

_____

WRITE IT

On a separate sheet of paper, write a beginning for a story. Write about a trip into space. Then write about a problem that you could solve in your story.

A Story Plot

Tell when each event happened. Write <u>beginning</u>, <u>middle</u>, or <u>ending</u>.

1. Cinderella lived happily ever after. _____

2. Cinderella wanted to go to the ball. _____

3. She left the ball at midnight. _____

 A **plot** is the series of events in a story. It tells what happens. It tells the beginning, middle, and ending.

A. Write <u>beginning</u>, <u>middle</u>, or <u>ending</u> to tell in which part of the story each event belongs. The first one is done for you.

1. The other ducks laughed at the ugly little bird. _____middle_____

2. The ugly duck went out alone into the world. _____

3. The ugly little duck turned into a beautiful bird. _____

4. Cute ducks and one ugly one were born to mother duck. _____

5. The ugly duck spent a cold, hard winter. _____

B. Write <u>beginning</u>, <u>middle</u>, or <u>ending</u> to tell in which part of the story each event belongs. The first one is done for you.

6. The runners raced on Saturday morning. _____middle_____

7. Jody decided to enter the race. _____

8. Jody passed the finish line first! _____

9. Soon they were running around the track. _____

10. Another runner was right behind her. _____

11. Jody moved quickly ahead. _____

12. Jody ran as hard as she could. _____

NAME _____

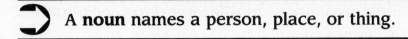

Writing with Nouns

⊃ A **noun** names a person, place, or thing.

A. Underline the nouns in each sentence.

1. The buildings almost touch the clouds.

2. Cars crawl slowly down the street.

3. Drivers noisily honk their horns.

4. The girl enjoys the busy city.

B. Circle the five nouns in the puzzle. Then write one noun in each sentence.

m	o	t	h	e	r
w	c	p	l	v	s
i	b	e	f	m	d
n	u	o	l	z	e
d	k	p	o	v	s
o	j	l	o	y	k
w	q	e	r	u	n

5. Lee rides the elevator to the top

_____ .

6. He visits his _____ in the office.

7. She works at her _____ .

8. They look out the _____ .

9. How tiny the _____ look!

C. Write a noun to complete each sentence.

10. The tall buildings are in the _____ .

11. This busy place has many _____ .

12. A _____ sells hot dogs at a stand.

13. The children visit a _____ .

WRITE IT

Name a place you like to visit. Write a list of the people, places, and things you can see there. Write on a separate sheet of paper.

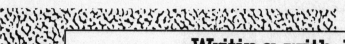

Writing with Nouns

Complete each sentence. Write the noun <u>farmer</u>, <u>farm</u>, or <u>potatoes</u>. Use each clue in ( ) to help you.

1. I am a _____ . (names a person)

2. I live on a _____ . (names a place)

3. I like _____ . (names a thing)

 A **noun** names a person, place, or thing.

A. Write each word that is a noun. Use the words from the list. The first one is done for you.

| sister | sell | dog | barn | field | sharpen |
| carry | country | fence | driver | cow | wheat |

1. _____sister_____   4. _____   7. _____

2. _____   5. _____   8. _____

3. _____   6. _____   9. _____

B. Complete each sentence. Write the correct noun from the box.

| man pie vegetable car family basket village |

EXAMPLE: A _____car_____ stops in front of the farm.

10. A _____ opened the car door.

11. He held a _____ of potatoes.

12. I live in the next _____ .

13. My _____ will have a surprise for dinner.

14. I will bake a pumpkin _____ tonight.

15. Potatoes are my favorite _____ .

Singular Nouns and Plural Nouns

A **singular noun** names one person, place, or thing. A **plural noun** names more than one person, place, or thing. Add **-s** to form the plural of most nouns.

A. Underline the singular noun in each sentence. Circle the plural noun.

1. Trucks stop in front of the store.

2. The drivers deliver food.

3. A woman opens the doors.

4. The jars go on each shelf.

B. Complete the puzzle. Write the plural form of each noun in ( ). Start the first word in square 5.

5. A woman buys three red _____ . (apple)

6. She checks both _____ in her hands. (list)

7. Two _____ of soup fall to the floor. (can)

8. A girl wants some _____ . (peanut)

9. A boy packs the food in _____ . (bag)

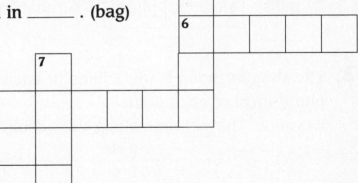

WRITE IT

Write about a trip to a market. Use both singular and plural nouns to name persons, places, and things. Write on a separate sheet of paper.

Singular Nouns and Plural Nouns

Circle each noun that describes things in the picture.

Singular Nouns	Plural Nouns
shell	shells
shovel	shovels
pail	pails

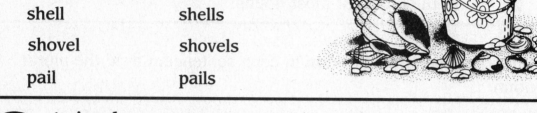

 A **singular noun** names one person, place, or thing. A **plural noun** names more than one person, place, or thing. Add -s to form the plural of most nouns.

A. Circle <u>singular</u> if the noun is singular. Circle <u>plural</u> if the noun is plural.

EXAMPLE: turtles

singular	plural

1. tents	singular	plural	4. buckets	singular	plural
2. crab	singular	plural	5. pigeons	singular	plural
3. gulls	singular	plural	6. chair	singular	plural

B. The singular noun is underlined in each sentence pair. Write the plural form of each noun.

EXAMPLE: The <u>girl</u> runs along the beach.

The _____girls_____ run along the beach.

7. The <u>wave</u> hits the beach.

The _____ hit the beach.

8. My mother builds a <u>castle</u> in the sand.

My mother builds _____ in the sand.

Spelling Plural Nouns

⟳ Add -es to form the plural of nouns that end in ss, x, ch, or sh. If a noun ends in a consonant and y, change the y to i and add -es to form the plural.

A. Write the plural form of each singular noun.

1. woman _____   3. peach _____

2. baby _____   4. ax _____

B. Write the plural form of the noun in ( ). Write one letter on each line.

5. What is in those long, thin (box)?   ◯ __ __ __ __

6. You may have three (guess).   __ ◯ __ __ __ __ __

7. They are eight (inch) long.   __ __ __ ◯ __ __

8. They do not have (foot).   __ __ ◯ __

9. They do not smell like (daisy).   __ __ __ __ __ __ ◯

10. They are not round like (dish).   __ __ ◯ __ __

11. You cannot eat them like (berry).   __ __ ◯ __ __ __

C. Write the circled letters. Put each letter on the line above the sentence number. The first one is done for you.

Six paint $\dfrac{b}{5}$ __ __ __ __ __ __ are in the boxes.
　　　　　　5　11　6　9　7　8　10

WRITE IT

Think of singular nouns that end in ss, x, ch, sh, and y. Write a riddle that is answered by the plural form of at least one of the words. Write the answer to the riddle. Write on a separate sheet of paper.

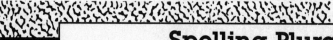

Spelling Plural Nouns

Look at the chart. Read the plural nouns. Circle the letters that have been changed or added. The first one is done for you.

Singular Nouns	Rule	Plural Nouns
glass	add -es	glass(es)
box	add -es	boxes
watch	add -es	watches
dish	add -es	dishes
city	change y to i and add -es	cities

 Add -es to form the plural of nouns that end in ss, x, ch, or sh. If a noun ends in a consonant and y, change the y to i and add -es to form the plural.

A. Draw a line from each singular noun to the plural form of the noun. The first one is done for you.

1. pony   foxes   5. hobby   inches

2. man   men   6. foot   classes

3. fox   wishes   7. class   hobbies

4. wish   ponies   8. inch   feet

B. Write each sentence. Use the plural form of the noun in ( ).

EXAMPLE: Rover rests under the _____bushes_____ . (bush)

9. Then he sees the _____ . (butterfly)

10. He runs over our _____ . (lunch)

11. The _____ of juice spill. (glass)

12. But the _____ are fine. (sandwich)

Singular Possessive Nouns

⊃ A **possessive noun** shows ownership. To form the possessive of a singular noun, add an apostrophe and <u>s</u> (<u>'s</u>).

A. Use the possessive form of each noun in ( ). Write each word group in the blank.

1. (boy) breakfast _____

2. (puppy) dish _____

3. (student) snack _____

4. (Mrs. Clark) soup _____

5. (baker) pans _____

6. (Jody) sandwich _____

7. (Fluffy) milk _____

8. (Aunt Mary) fork _____

B. The possessive noun is written incorrectly in each sentence. Write each sentence correctly.

9. Sallys bread tasted delicious.

_____

10. She baked it for her cousins party.

_____

11. Sally followed her aunts recipe.

_____

WRITE IT

Write sentences about a party you enjoyed. Use some possessive nouns. Write on a separate sheet of paper.

Singular Possessive Nouns

Match each word group that has the same meaning. Draw a line to connect the word groups.

1. the tail of the <u>cat</u>   Jan's toy

2. the toy that belongs to <u>Jan</u>   the cat's tail

 A **singular noun** names one person, place, or thing. A **possessive noun** shows ownership. To form the possessive of a singular noun, add an apostrophe and <u>s</u> ('<u>s</u>).

A. Circle the possessive noun in each sentence. Then write it in the blank. The first one is done for you.

1. (Mr. Flint's) class made toy animals. _____ Mr. Flint's _____

2. Jenny's toy is a green parrot. _____

3. The parrot's eyes are orange. _____

4. Miko's elephant is funny. _____

5. Miko put the dress on the
   elephant's body. _____

B. Rewrite each sentence below. Use the possessive form of the underlined noun.

Example: <u>Frank</u> spider was made of wire.
          Frank's spider was made of wire.

6. The <u>spider</u> web was made of string.

_____

7. Long ears were put on <u>Hector</u> rabbit.

_____

8. He used a soft ball for the <u>rabbit</u> tail.

_____

Plural Possessive Nouns

⊃ To form the possessive of a plural noun that ends in <u>s</u>, add an apostrophe (').

A. The signs at the zoo are written incorrectly. Each one should have a plural possessive noun. Write the possessive form.

| seals pool | alligators island | tigers house | birds cage |

1. _____   3. _____

2. _____   4. _____

B. Rewrite each sentence. Use the possessive form of the underlined plural noun.

5. The <u>lions</u> roars are very loud.

_____

6. People laugh at the <u>monkeys</u> tricks.

_____

7. Children ride on the <u>horses</u> backs.

_____

8. We pet the animals in the <u>lambs</u> pen.

_____

9. The lambs eat from the <u>twins</u> hands.

_____

WRITE IT

Write sentences about zoo animals. Use plural nouns, such as the possessive form of <u>bears' claws</u> or <u>giraffes' spots</u>. Write on a separate sheet of paper.

NAME _____

Plural Possessive Nouns

Read each sentence below. The apostrophe (') makes the plural noun show ownership. Underline each word that shows ownership.

1. The birds' feathers are shiny. **2.** The wind blew the girls' hats.

→ Most plural nouns end in <u>s</u>. To form the possessive of a plural noun that ends in <u>s</u>, add an apostrophe (').

A. Circle the plural possessive noun in each word group. Write it in the blank. The first one is done for you.

1. (cousins') hats _____cousins'_____ 5. planes' pilots _____

2. babies' bottles _____ 6. sharks' fins _____

3. goats' tails _____ 7. trucks' wheels _____

4. flowers' stems _____ 8. ducks' bills _____

B. Complete each sentence. Use the possessive form of each plural noun in ( ).

EXAMPLE: My _____friends'_____ pictures were in a show. (friends)

9. The _____ dresses were green. (dancers)

10. We laughed at the _____ tricks. (monkeys)

11. The _____ buttons glowed in the dark. (clowns)

12. The _____ trunks were long. (elephants)

13. The _____ voices were happy. (singers)

14. The _____ laughter filled the room. (girls)

15. The _____ music was loud. (bands)

Grade 3, Unit 2, Lesson 5
GRAMMAR and MECHANICS: Possessive Nouns (Reteaching)

© SILVER BURDETT GINN INC.

30

Compounds

A. Complete each sentence by writing a compound word. Use two words in the sentence to form the compound. Underline the two words.

1. A bath for a bird is a _____.

2. The tip of a finger is a _____.

3. A pole for a flag is a _____.

4. The side of a hill is a _____.

5. A room with a bed is a _____.

6. The day of your birth is your _____.

7. A ball you throw into a basket is a _____.

8. A pen babies play in is a _____.

9. Work you do at home is _____.

10. If you get sick at sea, you are _____.

11. A pad worn on the knee is a _____.

12. A yard outside a barn is a _____.

B. Use the words in each row to form two different compounds. Write them in the blanks.

13. fire   fly   place   _____   _____

14. snow   man   ball   _____   _____

15. coat   rain   bow   _____   _____

16. dog   light   house   _____   _____

17. hall   way   drive   _____   _____

18. blue   straw   berries   _____   _____

Compounds

A compound is a word formed from two or more smaller words. Write the two smaller words that form each compound below.

_____ + _____ = doorbell   _____ + _____ = pancake

A. Complete the puzzle. Use the picture clues to write compound words. The first one is done for you.

DOWN

1.   4.

2.    5.

3.   6.

ACROSS

7.   8.

B. Find the compound word in each sentence below. Then write the two words that form each compound. The first one is done for you.

9. The countryside is pleasant.   _____country_____ _____side_____

10. Flowers grow on the hillside.   _____ _____

11. A bluebird sings in a tree.   _____ _____

12. Blueberries grow on the bushes.   _____ _____

A Paragraph

> A **paragraph** is a group of sentences about one main idea. The first word of a paragraph is indented.

A. Read each paragraph. Write the main idea.

1.   The first movie ever shown was different from movies of today. It was shown in 1895 and had no sound. It was a silent movie. Words on the screen helped tell the story.

_____

2.   Many popular movie stars acted in the early movies. Stars of funny movies included Charlie Chaplin, Buster Keaton, and the Keystone Cops. Tom Mix and William S. Hart played cowboys.

_____

3.   The Jazz Singer was the first movie with sound. The film was made in 1927. It starred Al Jolson. He sang some songs in the movie. People liked The Jazz Singer very much.

_____

B. Complete the sentence so that it tells a main idea. Then finish writing the paragraph.

    Most movies on television _____

_____

_____

_____

WRITE IT

On a separate sheet of paper, write about a movie you saw. When you are finished, check to see that each sentence is about your main idea.

A Paragraph

Read the paragraph. Then circle what the sentences below tell about.

Birds sing as a way of talking to each other. Male birds sing more than female birds. They sing to have females notice them. They sing to keep other birds away from their tree.

1. female birds   **2.** birds singing   **3.** fighting songs

A **paragraph** is a group of sentences about one main idea. The first word of a paragraph is indented, or moved in.

A. Write the group of sentences below as a paragraph.

    1. Sea gulls live near the water.

    2. They live near oceans, lakes, and rivers.

    3. Gulls will follow a ship at sea.

    4. They like the food thrown from the ship.

_____

_____

_____

B. Write the sentence that tells the main idea of each paragraph.

    EXAMPLE: (from paragraph A above) ___Sea gulls live near the water.___

    5.   A homing pigeon carries messages. When taken far from its nest, it flies back home. It carries a message in a small tube. The tube is attached to the bird's leg.

_____

    6.   An owl has unusual feathers. The feathers around its eyes make it look wise. An owl can puff its feathers. This makes the owl look twice its size. Its soft feathers also help it fly silently.

_____

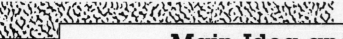

Main Idea and Details

 The **topic sentence** tells the main idea of the paragraph. The other sentences add details about the main idea.

A. Write the topic sentence of each paragraph. Underline the sentences that tell details.

1. My favorite sport is cheerleading. My friends and I lead cheers at basketball games. We have so much school spirit! We clap and yell. We get the fans to cheer for our team.

    _____

2. One jump I learned is the Herkie. It is named after L. R. Herkimer. For this jump, keep one leg bent back. Keep the other leg straight. Be sure to point your toes.

    _____

B. For each topic sentence, write one sentence that tells a detail.

3. People of all ages can enjoy bicycle riding.

    _____

4. A pool is a good place to swim.

    _____

5. It takes practice to be a good skater.

    _____

WRITE IT

On a separate sheet of paper, write about your favorite sport. Underline the topic sentence in your paragraph. Be sure to include sentences that give details about it.

Main Idea and Details

How many sentences tell about the main idea in dark print? _____

Did you know that you eat different parts of plants? You are eating roots when you eat a carrot. You are eating leaves when you eat lettuce. You are eating seeds when you eat peas.

 A paragraph has one main idea. The **topic sentence** tells the main idea of the paragraph. The other sentences add details about the main idea.

A. Match each **topic sentence** to a detail sentence. The first one is done for you.

Topic Sentences	Detail Sentences
1. Green plants make their food in their leaves.	• They may grow it in a garden.
2. There are many ways people get their food.	• Leaves need sunlight to make food.
3. Some green plants grow in the desert.	• The cactus stores water in its stem.

B. The sentence in dark type tells the main idea. Underline the sentences that add details about it. The first one is done for you.

4. **Some plants give off light, or glow in the dark.**

    Some glowing plants shine with an orange light.

    Some shine with a green light.

    Plants do not walk, but they do move.

5. **Several kinds of plants glow.**

    Many plants that live in the ocean glow.

    One kind of fig tree grows in hot, damp places.

    Some little plants that live on dead wood glow.

A Friendly Letter

➲ A **friendly letter** has five parts: the heading, greeting, body, closing, and signature.

A. Circle the letters that should be capitals. Add commas.

1. dear jenny
2. i am fine.
3. ryan

4. provo utah
5. your friend
6. i miss you.

7. may 3 1990
8. dear grandpa
9. sincerely yours

B. Rewrite the letter below correctly. Then write the names of the letter parts in the boxes.

72 shore drive
larchmont, new york 10538
april 8 1990

dear uncle ben thank you for the gift. i can't wait to read the book.
love abby

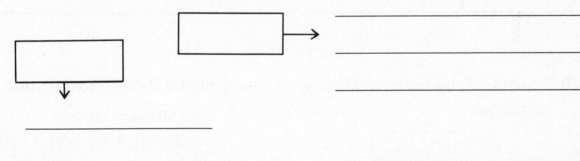

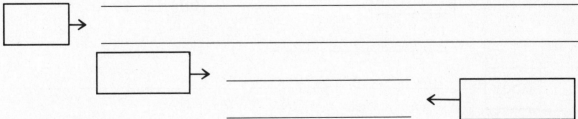

WRITE IT

Write a letter thanking someone for something. Write on a separate sheet of paper.

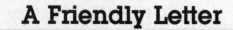

A Friendly Letter

The words in the boxes name each part of a friendly letter. Circle the four places where commas appear.

Greeting

Heading →
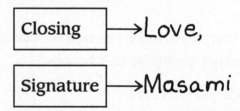
Route 2
Los Gatos, CA 95030
July 5, 1990

Dear Jose,

Body → Camp is great! I like swimming in the lake. Last night we made a campfire. We sang songs.

Closing →Love,

Signature →Masami

⟩ A **friendly letter** has five parts: the heading tells the writer's address and the date. The greeting says "hello." The body is the main part. The closing says "good-bye." The signature tells the writer's name.

A. Complete the letter to Masami. Add a greeting, body, closing, and signature.

32 Howard Street
Babylon, New York 11702
July 12, 1990

Greeting
↓
_____

Body → _____

_____

← Closing

_____

Signature → _____

Common Nouns and Proper Nouns

A **common noun** names any person, place, or thing. A **proper noun** names a particular person, place, or thing.

A. Circle each common noun. Underline each proper noun.

1. Hawaii is a very beautiful state.

2. Our plane flew over the Pacific Ocean.

3. Ann Ning likes to jog along the beach

4. Diamond Head is a famous lifeless volcano.

5. Maui was formed by two volcanic mountains.

6. Did your friend visit Hawaii Volcanoes National Park?

B. Underline the nouns in the note. Then write them on the chart.

Tracy,
 Hawaii has many islands. Aunt Jo lives on Oahu. Her cat is named Mr. Meow. Honolulu is the largest city. It is also the capital.

Common Nouns	**Proper Nouns**
_____	_____
_____	_____
_____	_____
_____	_____

WRITE IT

Write about a place you would like to visit. Use common nouns and proper nouns in your sentences. Write on a separate sheet of paper.

Common Nouns and Proper Nouns

Look at the pictures. Give the girl and the school a name. Write one of these names: <u>Franklin School</u>, <u>Peggy Jones</u>.

girl

school

_____

➡ A **noun** names a person, place, or thing. A **common noun** names any person, place, or thing. A **proper noun** names a particular person, place, or thing.

A. Write a proper noun for each common noun. Use the proper nouns from the box. The first one is done for you.

| Chicago   Buttons   Rosa Ortiz   Sunnyside Museum |

1. woman ___Rosa Ortiz___   3. museum _____

2. city _____   4. dog _____

B. Write the underlined common nouns and proper nouns in the correct group below. The first sentence is done for you.

5. <u>Utah</u> has many interesting <u>places</u>.

6. <u>Great Salt Lake</u> is saltier than the <u>ocean</u>.

7. Some large <u>rocks</u> look like <u>cities</u>.

Common Nouns

_____places_____   _____

_____   _____

Proper Nouns

_____Utah_____   _____

Names and Titles

➲ Each word in the name of a person or pet begins with a capital letter.

A. Circle each name that is written correctly.

1. mr. Chin quan   4. Carol T. Little   7. Felipe Rosado

2. Ms. Carmen Cruz   5. Mr. george jenkins   8. dr ann s johnson

3. Mr. Taro Matsuo   6. Snowy   9. mrs joan park

B. Write correctly the names you did not circle above.

10. _____   12. _____

11. _____   13. _____

C. Look at each picture. Then write the name that answers each question. Write the name correctly.

mr c f sanders

henry g adams

ms terry wright

14. Who is driving? _____

15. Who is reading? _____

16. Who is cooking? _____

WRITE IT

Write your name using a title. Then write the names and titles of people you like. Write on a separate sheet of paper.

Names and Titles

Write the title and name for each person. Write the name of the pet.

Dr. J. Rogers   Wags   Mrs. Ana Torres

_____   _____   _____

The names of people and pets are proper nouns. Each word in the name of a person or pet begins with a capital letter.

A. Circle each name that is written correctly.

EXAMPLE: (Mr. Chen Ping)

1. Rose M. Park   4. Julio p. Santos   7. Miss Holly brown

2. mrs. Betsy Lewis   5. Dr. Kate Minelli   8. S J goldberg

3. Mr. Marvin Carr   6. chewie   9. Ms. Linda Tell

B. Write each name correctly. The first one is done for you.

10. miss dolly diaz   Miss Dolly Diaz _____

11. dr gerry goodhealth   _____

12. mr billy baker   _____

13. ms polly pickles   _____

14. sniffy   _____

15. mr frank lee   _____

16. mrs sandy shore   _____

Place Names

⊃ Each word in the name of a street, town, city, or state begins with a capital letter.

A. Circle the place name on each road sign. Then write each name correctly on a line below.

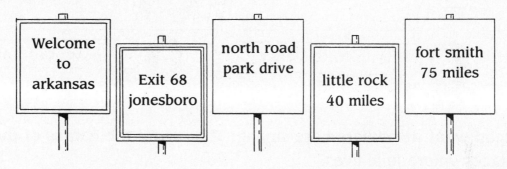

Welcome
to
arkansas

Exit 68
jonesboro

north road
park drive

little rock
40 miles

fort smith
75 miles

1. _____   4. _____

2. _____   5. _____

3. _____   6. _____

B. Write each place name correctly in a blank.

7. _____

8. _____

9. _____

10. _____

11. _____

12. _____

WRITE IT

Write the name of your street, city, and state. Then write the names of other streets, cities, and states where you have friends or family. Write on a separate sheet of paper.

Place Names

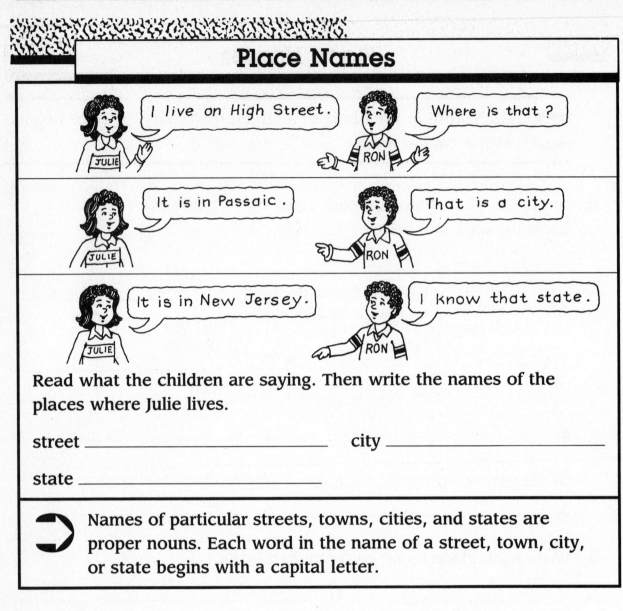

Read what the children are saying. Then write the names of the places where Julie lives.

street _____   city _____

state _____

⊃ Names of particular streets, towns, cities, and states are proper nouns. Each word in the name of a street, town, city, or state begins with a capital letter.

A. Circle each place name that is written correctly. The first one is done for you.

1. (Boston)   2. minnesota   3. maple Street   4. New Hampshire

   boston   Minnesota   Maple Street   New hampshire

B. Write each place name in ( ) correctly in each sentence. The first one is done for you.

5. My family just moved to _____Ann Arbor_____ . (ann arbor)

6. It is in the state of _____ . (michigan)

7. We bought a house on _____ . (oak drive)

Calendar Words

➲ The name of a day or a month begins with a capital letter. Each word in the name of a holiday or a special day begins with a capital letter.

A. Circle the letter that should be capitalized in each sentence. Rewrite the word correctly.

1. On sunday we arrived in Washington, D. C. _____

2. On monday we saw planes and balloons. _____

3. We saw toys from long ago on tuesday. _____

4. We saw part of the White House on wednesday. _____

5. We saw dinosaur bones on thursday. _____

B. Write each month, holiday, or special day correctly.

october	february	thanksgiving	valentine's day
january	november	new year's day	halloween

Month

6. _____

7. _____

8. _____

9. _____

Holiday or Special Day

10. _____

11. _____

12. _____

13. _____

WRITE IT

Choose a city you would like to visit. Write your schedule on a separate sheet of paper. Write the month, day of the week, and place you will visit.

Calendar Words

Find your birthday on a calendar. Write the name of the month you were born. Be sure to write a capital for the first letter.

My birthday is in _____ .

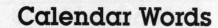 **Calendar words** are proper nouns. The name of a day or month begins with a capital letter. Each word in the name of a holiday or special day begins with a capital letter.

A. The name of each day, month, and holiday is underlined. Write each name correctly.

EXAMPLE: I watch television on <u>saturday</u>. ___Saturday___

1. Walt Disney was born in <u>december</u>.

2. A new Disney movie can be seen on <u>friday</u>.

3. Some Disney characters are in parades on <u>thanksgiving</u>.

4. I saw two Disney movies in <u>june</u>.

_____   _____

_____   _____

B. Write each day, month, holiday, or special day correctly.

EXAMPLE: independence day ___Independence Day___

5. june   8. wednesday

_____   _____

6. easter   9. tuesday

_____   _____

7. sunday   10. labor day

_____   _____

Context Clues

A. Read each pair of sentences. Write what you think the underlined word means.

1. The whole country likes baseball. It is a <u>national</u> favorite.

   _____

2. Someone shouts to start the game. He <u>cries</u>, "Play ball!"

   _____

3. Many people go to baseball games. In all, over thirty million people <u>attend</u> games.

   _____

4. Mrs. Moreno is highly interested in baseball. She is a baseball <u>fan</u>. _____

5. People filled the <u>stadium</u> where the game was held.

   _____

6. The batter hit the ball and ran to first base. She hit a <u>single</u>!

   _____

7. The runner <u>tumbled</u>. He fell as he ran to the base.

   _____

B. Complete each sentence with a word that makes sense. Use context clues to help you.

   We went to a baseball game. The teams were on the

   _____ . The pitcher _____ the ball.

The _____ hit the ball and ran to first

_____ . He was safe! The _____

cheered.

Context Clues

A clue that helps you understand a new word is called a **context clue**. Circle the word or words that help you understand the underlined word in each sentence below.

1. I took a <u>rapid</u> train to New York. The fast trip took four minutes.

2. The train came to a <u>gradual</u>, not sudden, stop.

A. Read each sentence. Circle the meaning of the underlined word. Use context clues to help you. The first one is done for you.

1. The <u>timid</u> child clung to her father and would not talk.

   (shy)   loud

2. The <u>cast</u> of the show is great! The people are wonderful actors.

   people in a show   people watching a show

3. Do not hike in the <u>swamp</u> without boots.

   dry land   wet land

4. The <u>herd</u> ran to the barn. Thunder had scared the cows.

   a group of plants   a group of animals

5. The <u>shrill</u>, sharp sound of a whistle woke me.

   piercing, high   soft, sweet

B. Read each sentence below. Write what you think the underlined word means. The first one is done for you.

6. The train <u>station</u> is in the city. The trains stop there.

   place where trains stop

7. The airplane waits on the <u>runway</u> until it can take off.

   _____

8. Airplanes are usually <u>prompt</u>, or on time. _____

Couplets

 A **couplet** is two lines that rhyme, one after the other.

A. Read the following poem. Then follow the directions.

Watching the Moon

September evenings such as these
The moon hides early in the trees,
And when we drive along the shore
I think I miss the trees the more
Because the moon is coming down
Beyond the branches and will drown.

—*David McCord*

1. Write the number of couplets. _____

2. Write the pairs of rhyming words.

_____

_____

3. Why does the poet think the moon will drown?

_____

B. Read the line below. Write a new line to make a couplet.

Sometimes when I've gone to bed

_____

WRITE IT

Write your own couplet. You can use the rhyming words below.
You can use other rhyming words, too. Write on a separate sheet of
paper.

day/play   fun/done   time/climb   fast/last

Couplets

Read the poem. It has two couplets.

Mirrors

The sun must have a lot of **fun**
from dawn of day till day is **done**, ⎤ couplet 1

Seeing its bright and shiny **face**
in every puddle every **place**. ⎤ couplet 2

— *Aileen Fisher*

How many lines are in each couplet? _____
Do the words in dark type rhyme? _____
Do the rhyming lines come one after the other? _____

 Poets often use couplets in their poems. A **couplet** is two lines that rhyme, one after the other.

A. Read the following poem. Next to it draw a picture of some shoes you like. Then answer the questions.

What is the opposite of a *shoe*?
Either the *right* or *left* will **do**,
Depending on which one you've **got**.
The question's foolish, is it **not**?

— *Richard Wilbur*

1. How many pairs of rhyming words are there is this poem? _____
2. What word in the poem rhymes with each word below?

shoe _____   got _____

B. Finish this rhyme to make a couplet.

I smiled at the girl, and I heard her say

Will you come out and _____ ?

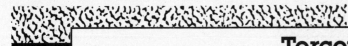

Tercets

⟳ A **tercet** is a poem of three lines that rhyme. You can write tercets with different rhyming patterns.

A. Write the rhyming pattern next to each line in the tercet. (Hint: Each poem has one of these patterns: <u>AAA</u>, <u>ABB</u>)

1. from "Stars" by Carolyn Hancock

Little stars have five sharp wings,   _____

And they fly   _____

Up in the sky.   _____

2. "The People" by Elizabeth Madox Roberts

The ants are walking under the ground,   _____

And the pigeons are flying over the steeple,   _____

And in between are the people.   _____

3. from "Moon" by William Jay Smith

I have a white cat whose name is Moon;   _____

He eats catfish from a wooden spoon,   _____

And sleeps till five each afternoon.   _____

B. Complete the tercet. Use any rhyming pattern you wish.

The sun is shining everywhere.

_____

_____

WRITE IT

Write your own tercet about the outdoors. Use one of the following rhyming patterns: <u>AAA</u>, <u>AAB</u>, or <u>BBA</u>. Write on a separate sheet of paper.

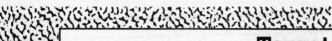

Tercets

Read the tercets below.

Down! Down!	from **Climbing**
Down, down!	The trunk of a tree
Yellow and brown	is the road for me
The leaves are falling over the town.	on a sunny summer day.
— *Eleanor Farjeon*	— *Aileen Fisher*

1. How many lines are in each tercet? _____
2. Do all the lines rhyme in the tercet on the left? _____
3. Do all the lines rhyme in the tercet on the right? _____

 A **tercet** is a poem of three lines that rhyme. You can write tercets with different rhyming patterns.

A. Read the poem. Then follow the directions.

Winter Night

It is very dark	Bushes are first
But not late.	As flakes fall,
Not after eight.	Then the top of a wall.
The only light	What used to be dark
Comes from snow	Is now a hill.
Beginning to show.	It is very still.

— *Harry Behn*

1. Write the number of tercets in the poem. _____
2. Write the rhyming words.

_____

B. Complete the tercet with a rhyming line or one that does not rhyme.

The sky is light.
The sun is bright.

Let's go _____

Writing with Pronouns

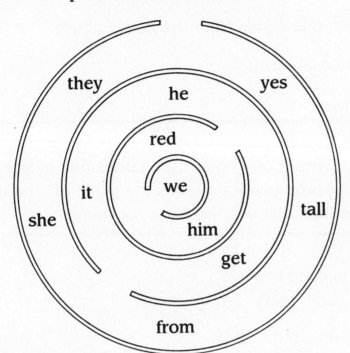

⟩ A **pronoun** takes the place of a noun or nouns.

A. Follow the pronouns until you reach the center of the circle. Then write the pronouns on the lines.

they   he   yes

red

it   we

she   tall

him

get

from

1. _____

2. _____

3. _____

4. _____

5. _____

6. _____

B. Write a pronoun to replace the underlined noun or nouns.

7. <u>The tickets</u> are for sale.   _____

8. <u>Taro and I</u> sell them.   _____

9. <u>Luisa</u> buys two tickets.   _____

10. She waits near the clock for <u>Jim</u>.   _____

11. The <u>play</u> starts in five minutes.   _____

12. <u>Taro</u> closes the big doors.   _____

WRITE IT

Write about a play or story you like. Write sentences that use pronouns. Write on a separate sheet of paper.

Writing with Pronouns

Singular Pronouns	Plural Pronouns
I she it her you he me him	we they them you us

Complete each sentence. Use words from the boxes above.

1. _____ found the pencils.

2. Jill found _____ .

 A **pronoun** takes the place of a noun or nouns. A **singular pronoun** takes the place of a noun that names one person, place, or thing. A **plural pronoun** takes the place of a noun that names more than one person, place, or thing.

A. Circle two pronouns in each row.

EXAMPLE: Lisa (me) tall very (you) next

1. see   her   get   we   red   desk
2. he   Mark   maybe   cat   now   I
3. but   you   it   joy   key   hope
4. rug   home   play   him   Rita   they

B. Circle the pronoun in each sentence. Write it in the space.

EXAMPLE:(She)buys stamps from a machine.   _____She_____

5. They write letters to Billy.   _____

6. Matthew puts them in an envelope.   _____

7. He addresses the envelope.   _____

8. Alice puts it in the mailbox.   _____

9. We watch the envelope drop.   _____

Subject Pronouns

 The words I, you, she, he, it, we, and they are **subject pronouns**.

A. Circle the subject pronoun in each sentence. Write it in the space.

1. We have a new library in our town. _____

2. It is open six days a week. _____

3. She is the new teacher. _____

4. I look for a book about tigers. _____

5. He reads the animal books. _____

6. They are kept on the bottom shelf. _____

B. The subject of each sentence is underlined. Circle the subject pronoun in ( ) that can take its place.

7. The door opens at nine o'clock. (I, It, They)

8. The people climb the library steps. (They, He, She)

9. Mrs. Ryan meets the children. (He, She, It)

10. José and I listen to a story. (You, They, We)

11. Nina and Judy take out records. (We, They, I)

12. Julie reads a book. (He, She, We)

13. Steve stamps the children's books. (She, He, You)

14. Izumi has four books. (She, It, I)

15. Brian and I ride our bikes home. (They, We, You)

16. Mr. Bolivar takes Frank home. (She, I, He)

WRITE IT

Write about a visit to a library. Write sentences that use subject pronouns. Write on a separate sheet of paper.

Subject Pronouns

Write subjects for sentences 2 and 4. Use pronouns that match the pictures.

1. Luis bakes bread.   **3.** Lina bakes bread.

2. _____ bakes bread.   **4.** _____ bakes bread.

 The subject of a sentence names someone or something. The words I, you, she, he, it, we, and they are **subject pronouns**.

A. Each subject that has a noun is underlined. Circle the subject pronouns.

EXAMPLE: The bowl is ready. (It) is ready.

1. Max beats the eggs. He beats the eggs.

2. Dave and Ellen mix the batter. They mix the batter.

3. The bread goes into the pan. It goes into the pan.

4. The children watch. They watch.

5. The batter rises. It rises.

6. Ellen prepares the oven. She prepares the oven.

B. Complete each sentence. Write the subject pronoun in ( ).

EXAMPLE: ___She___ cuts the bread. (Mrs. Cata, She)

7. _____ rings. (It, The doorbell)

8. _____ like the good smell. (Paco and Lee, They)

9. _____ takes a bite. (Paco, He)

Object Pronouns

The words <u>me</u>, <u>you</u>, <u>him</u>, <u>her</u>, <u>it</u>, <u>us</u>, and <u>them</u> are **object pronouns**. You can use object pronouns in the predicates of sentences.

A. Circle the object pronoun in each sentence. Write it in the blank.

1. The children bring the shells to us.   _____

2. Carlos likes to gather them.   _____

3. Mia likes to go with him.   _____

4. The children find them along the beach.   _____

5. Mia shows me a long, thin shell.   _____

6. She holds it very carefully.   _____

B. Use one of the pronouns in the box for each underlined word or words. Write each new sentence.

them	it	us	him	her

7. Sam fills <u>a pail</u> with shells.

_____

8. Carlos fills <u>two pails</u> with shells.

_____

9. Judy fills a pail for <u>Sara</u>.

_____

WRITE IT

Write about the things you can find on a beach. Use object pronouns in some of your sentences. Write on a separate sheet of paper.

Object Pronouns

Match the sentences that have the same meaning.

1. The cat follows <u>Linda</u>.   The cat follows <u>them</u>.

2. The cat follows <u>Linda and me</u>.   The cat follows <u>it</u>.

3. The cat follows <u>the boys</u>.   The cat follows <u>her</u>.

4. The cat follows <u>the bike</u>.   The cat follows <u>us</u>.

Did you notice that the underlined words are in the predicate of each sentence?

> The words <u>me</u>, <u>you</u>, <u>him</u>, <u>her</u>, <u>it</u>, <u>us</u>, and <u>them</u> are **object pronouns**. Object pronouns take the place of words in the predicates of sentences.

A. Circle each object pronoun. Then write it. The first one is done for you.

mail	(me)	them	when	us	run	and
you	open	it	call	her	him	

1. ___me___   3. _____   5. _____   7. _____

2. _____   4. _____   6. _____

B. Circle the pronoun that completes each sentence correctly.

EXAMPLE: The bean seeds are for (he, (him)).

8. Ben helps (them, they) dig the garden.

9. Mom plants seeds in (we, it).

10. Dad waters (they, them) every day.

11. Ben shows (her, she) the clean yard.

12. Mom smiles at (him, he).

13. Beans make good salads for (we, us).

Possessive Pronouns

⟶ A **possessive pronoun** shows ownership.

A. Write the possessive pronoun from each sentence.

1. Sam likes to play his horn. _____

2. Molly beats her drum. _____

3. Their friends play in the band, too. _____

4. "Mrs. Wong is our leader," says Sam. _____

5. "Practice your instruments," says Mrs. Wong. _____

B. Circle the possessive pronoun in ( ) that takes the place of the underlined words. Then write each pronoun on the music stands.

6. Mary's teacher has a new piano. (His, Her, Its)

7. The movers delivered Mr. Lamb's piano last week. (his, her, its)

8. The movers' truck was very big. (His, Their, My)

9. The piano's keys are black and white and shiny. (Her, Your, Its)

10. The students' faces light up. (Their, Its, My)

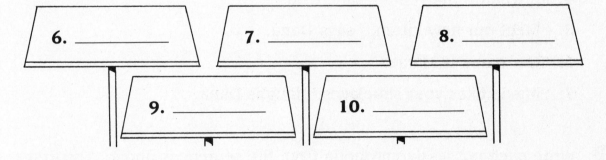

WRITE IT

Write about an instrument you like. Use some possessive pronouns. Write on separate paper.

Possessive Pronouns

| my | your | his | her | its | our | their |

Complete each sentence. Write a pronoun from the box.

The girl's hair is curly.

1. _____ hair is curly.

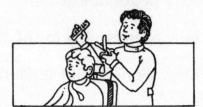

Mr. Vargas cuts the boy's hair.

2. Mr. Vargas cuts _____ hair.

 A **possessive pronoun** shows ownership. The words <u>my</u>, <u>your</u>, <u>his</u>, <u>her</u>, <u>its</u>, <u>our</u>, and <u>their</u> are possessive pronouns.

A. Circle the possessive pronoun in each sentence.
EXAMPLE: Dana waits for (her) uncle.

1. My uncle is coming to visit.

2. Uncle Nick drives his car from Boston.

3. Uncle Nick drives in front of their house.

4. Its windows have dark blue trim.

5. "Meet our new kitten," says Dana.

6. "Her name is Maxie."

7. "Maxie likes your shoelaces," laughs Dana.

B. Write each possessive pronoun from the sentences above. The first one is done for you.

8. __My__   10. _____   12. _____   14. _____

9. _____   11. _____   13. _____

USAGE

Using *I* and *me*

> Use I in the subject of a sentence. Use a capital letter for the word I. Use <u>me</u> in the predicate of a sentence.

A. Underline <u>I</u> or <u>me</u> in each sentence. Then circle <u>subject</u> or <u>predicate</u>.

1. Larry and I go to the post office.   subject   predicate

2. I see Mr. Green there.   subject   predicate

3. He waves to Larry and me.   subject   predicate

4. Mr. Green and I are neighbors.   subject   predicate

5. He lives next door to me.   subject   predicate

6. Mr. Green has known me a long time.   subject   predicate

7. I like Mrs. Green.   subject   predicate

B. Write <u>I</u> or <u>me</u> to complete each sentence. Each group of sentences describes a person in one of the pictures. Draw a line from the riddle to the name of the person.

8. _____ drive children to school.

   _____ say good morning to them.

   They say good morning to _____ .

Mr. Scott

9. The children show _____ their work.

   The children and _____ talk about it.

   They hand _____ their papers.

Mrs. Morrelli

WRITE IT

Write about what you might like to do when you grow up. Use <u>I</u> and <u>me</u> in your sentences. Write on a separate sheet of paper.

Using *I* and *me*

Complete the sentences. Use the words from the chart. Notice that a line separates each subject and predicate.

1. _____ I give Frisky a bath.

2. Frisky I splashes _____ .

Subject	Predicate
I	me

 Use the pronouns I and me to talk about yourself. Use I in the subject of a sentence. Use me in the predicate of a sentence.

A. Complete each sentence with I or me. Notice that a line separates each subject and predicate.

EXAMPLE: ____I____ I look for Frisky.

1. _____ I find Frisky under the bed.

2. He I hides from _____ .

3. Frisky I is not happy to see _____ .

4. _____ I carry Frisky into the yard.

5. Jan I opens the door for _____ .

6. _____ I take Frisky to the park.

B. Underline the words in ( ) that correctly complete each sentence.
EXAMPLE: (Jan and I) (Jan and me) put Frisky in the tub.

7. He tries to get away from (Jan and me) (me and Jan).

8. (Jan and I) (Jan and me) hold Frisky down.

9. Frisky splashes (Jan and me) (Jan and I).

10. (Jan and I) (I and Jan) quickly wash him.

11. (I and Jan) (Jan and I) are wet, too.

12. It is hard work for (Jan and I) (Jan and me).

Homophones

A. Match each homophone with its meaning.

1. wait   how heavy something is

2. weight   to stay until someone comes

3. male   a man or boy

4. mail   letters, packages sent by post

5. I   part of the body people see with

6. eye   the person who is talking or writing

7. week   seven days, one after another

8. weak   not strong

B. Each sentence below needs a pair of homophones. One is already there. Write the other homophone in the blank.

9. I have seen the last _____ of the play.

10. Joe set the table for _____ friends.

11. He blew up ten _____ balloons for the party.

12. Sarah and her friends ate _____ sandwiches.

13. One boy _____ a prize for winning a game.

14. He threw the ball _____ the hole.

15. Our friends stayed for an _____ .

16. Can you hear the music from _____?

17. I am coming to the party at _____ o'clock.

18. I will write to my cousin _____ now.

19. This knot is _____ tied well.

Homophones

Homophones are words that sound alike. They have different spellings and meanings. Underline the homophones in the sentence below.

What do you see on the deep blue sea?

A. Write the two homophones in each sentence. The first one is done for you.

1. He knows that a fly is on his nose.   _____knows_____   _____nose_____

2. Did you hear that Josh is here?   _____   _____

3. Would you help Frank carry the wood?   _____   _____

4. The tale is about a rabbit with a fluffy tail.   _____   _____

5. We rode down the road on an elephant!   _____   _____

6. They're leaving without their jackets.   _____   _____

7. The one with the blue hat won the race.   _____   _____

B. Choose the correct homophone from the words in ( ). Write it in the sentence. The first one is done for you.

8. Mr. Pak bought a bag of _____flour_____ for pancakes. (flower, flour)

9. A beautiful red _____ grew on the bush. (rows, rose)

10. A _____ buzzed near the picnic table. (bee, be)

11. Nara _____ with her friend. (rode, road)

12. The team will _____ in front of the gate. (meat, meet)

A Paragraph That Persuades

A **persuasive paragraph** gives an opinion and facts or reasons to support the opinion.

A. Read each opinion and fact. Underline the fact if it supports the opinion.

1. Opinion: Skating on wheels is better than skating on ice.
   Fact: You do not need to wait until the ice freezes.

2. Opinion: Walking is better than riding a bicycle.
   Fact: You can travel faster on a bicycle.

3. Opinion: Running is a sport for everyone.
   Fact: You can do it without special equipment.

4. Opinion: It is rewarding to reach the top of a mountain.
   Fact: It is cold on the top of the mountain.

5. Opinion: Football is a rough sport.
   Fact: Football players wear padding for protection.

B. Begin a paragraph with one of the opinions below. Then add sentences that give facts or reasons to support the opinion.

Fishing is a good way to spend a summer afternoon.

Gymnasts must be strong.

Ice skating is the best winter sport.

_____

_____

_____

_____

WRITE IT

Write a persuasive paragraph about a team sport. State an opinion about the sport in the first sentence. Then support your opinion with facts or reasons. Write on a separate sheet of paper.

A Paragraph That Persuades

Read Carla's paragraph. Then answer the questions.

    The circus is the greatest show in the world. It is lively and colorful. Something exciting is always happening. You will never be bored there.

1. What is Carla's opinion about the circus?

_____

2. What is one reason Carla gives to support her opinion?

_____

 A **persuasive paragraph** gives an opinion and reasons to support it.

A. Read the opinion in dark print. Then underline the sentence that supports it.

    EXAMPLE: **Clowns are the best part of the circus.**

<u>They always make people laugh.</u>   Monkeys can forget their tricks.

1. The circus is better than the zoo.
   More happens at the circus.   You can learn more at the zoo.

2. The lion tamer has the most dangerous job.
   The lions could forget a trick.   The lions might attack.

3. The band is too noisy.
   You can not hear the master of the ring.   It plays familiar songs.

B. The topic sentence of the paragraph states an opinion. Choose three sentences from the box that support the opinion. Write them in the paragraph. The first one is done for you.

Some sparkle and shine.	They have buttons.
They have many bright colors.	They have bows, glitter, and lace.

    Circus costumes are unusual. They have many bright colors.

_____

Using Commas

> Use a comma after <u>yes</u> or <u>no</u> at the beginning of a sentence. Use a comma after the name of a person spoken to. Use commas to separate words in a series of three or more words.

A. Add commas where they are needed.

B. Write a complete sentence to answer each question below. Begin each sentence with <u>Yes</u> or <u>No</u>. Do not forget the commas.

1. Do you like picnics?

_____

2. Do ants bother you during picnics?

_____

3. Do you like to play games at picnics?

_____

4. Will you have a picnic soon?

_____

WRITE IT

Write complete sentences about going to the beach. Use three things that go together in your sentences. Be sure to put commas where needed. Write on a separate sheet of paper.

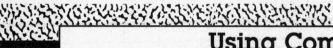

Using Commas

Read the sentences. Then answer the questions. Write the number of the correct sentence.

1. Sally Jean and Mike laughed.   **3.** No friends can play today.

2. Sally, Jean, and Mike laughed.   **4.** No, friends can play today.

         5. Bob Lee will go with you.

         6. Bob, Lee will go with you.

Which sentence tells about three people? _____

In which sentence is a person spoken to? _____

Which sentence tells you that friends can play today? _____

> Commas help make ideas clear. Use a comma after <u>yes</u> or <u>no</u> at the beginning of a sentence. Use a comma after the name of a person spoken to. Use commas to separate words in a series of three or more words.

Put commas in each sentence where they are needed. The first one is done for you.

1. Paul, Jim, and Eva read about Richard E. Byrd.

2. Kim do you know who Richard E. Byrd was?

3. Yes he was an explorer.

4. Byrd loved adventure travel and flying.

5. Lindsay do you remember what Byrd explored?

6. Yes he explored the North Pole and the South Pole.

7. Jim was Byrd the only child in his family?

8. No he had two brothers.

9. He traveled on boats sleds and airplanes.

10. Yes Byrd had an exciting life.

Writing with Verbs

 A word that shows action is a **verb**.

A. Discover the bird in the puzzle. First, underline the verb in each sentence. Then write each verb in the blanks.

1. Birds bring twigs to the tree.   __ __ __ __

2. They go among the branches.   __ __ __

3. They build a nest there.   __ __ __ __ __

4. The mother sits on the nest.   __ __ __ __

5. It sings to its baby birds.   __ __ __ __ __

B. Circle the verb in each sentence. Then write a new sentence using that verb.

6. The babies sleep in the nest.

_____

7. The mother bird flies to the ground.

_____

8. It finds food for its babies.

_____

9. The little birds open their mouths wide.

_____

WRITE IT

Write about a bird you have seen or read about. Use verbs to describe the bird's actions. Write on separate paper.

Writing with Verbs

Complete each sentence. Write a word that tells what students do. Use words from the box.

1. Students _____ in a classroom.

2. We _____ in our classroom.

Verbs
read   write   talk   draw

 A word that shows action is a **verb.** A verb tells what someone or something does.

A. Write the correct verb in each sentence. Use a verb from the box.

EXAMPLE: Maria _____jumps_____ rope.

1. Max _____ the ball.

2. Joe _____ the tree.

3. Lee _____ the boat.

4. Kelly _____ on her head.

5. Juan _____ a sand castle.

| climbs |
| stands |
| rows |
| builds |
| throws |
| jumps |

B. Circle the verb in each sentence. Write the verb in the blank.

EXAMPLE: The sun (shines) in the sky.   ___shines___

6. Dara opens the big picnic basket.   _____

7. The children sit on the yellow blanket.   _____

8. Joe pours the juice in paper cups.   _____

9. The children drink the cold juice.   _____

10. They pass the sandwiches and fruit.   _____

Verbs in the Present

→ A verb in the **present time** shows action that happens now. A present-time verb needs to agree with its subject.

A. Complete each sentence. Write the correct verb from the camera.

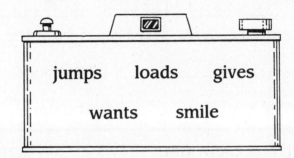

jumps   loads   gives

wants   smile

1. David's uncle _____ him a new camera.

2. David _____ it with film.

3. Three friends _____ for a picture.

4. Frisky _____ on Pat's lap.

5. The puppy _____ to be in the pictures, too.

B. Complete each sentence. Write the correct verb in ( ).

6. They _____ at the friendly puppy. (laugh, laughs)

7. We _____ into the camera. (stare, stares)

8. The new camera _____ softly. (click, clicks)

9. Frisky _____ under the sofa. (run, runs)

10. Lora _____ to the dog. (call, calls)

WRITE IT

Listen. A clock ticks. The wind blows. Write sentences that describe the sounds you hear. Use verbs in the present time. Write on a separate sheet of paper.

Verbs in the Present

Singular Noun	+	Present-Time Verb		Plural Noun	+	Present-Time Verb
girl		plays		girls		play
tree		grows		trees		grow
bird		sings		birds		sing

Complete each sentence. Write word pairs from the boxes.

1. One _____ _____ in the park.

2. Ten _____ _____ in the park.

 A verb in the **present time** shows action that happens now. A present-time verb needs to agree with its subject. Add -s or -es to the verb when the noun is singular.

A. Draw a line from the subject to the correct verb.

EXAMPLE: The whistle ———————— blow.
　　　　　The whistles ———————— blows.

1. The trumpet　　　　　　　　　　plays.

　 Six trumpets　　　　　　　　　　play.

2. One person　　　　　　　　　　march.

　 The people　　　　　　　　　　marches.

3. A child　　　　　　　　　　　　clap.

　 Children　　　　　　　　　　　claps.

B. Underline the correct verb in ( ). Then write the verb in the blank.

EXAMPLE: The marchers (<u>walk</u>, walks) to the music. ___walk___

4. The children (<u>wave</u>, waves) colorful flags. _____

5. The flags (<u>flap</u>, flaps) in the wind. _____

Using Pronouns and Verbs That Agree

> A verb in the present time must agree with the pronoun used in the subject of a sentence.

A. Complete each sentence. Write the correct verb in ( ).

1. He _____ the bucket of corn. (get, gets)

2. It _____ five pounds. (weigh, weighs)

3. We _____ six pink pigs. (feed, feeds)

4. They _____ a big meal. (eat, eats)

5. She _____ the barn door. (open, opens)

6. You _____ the hen's eggs. (gather, gathers)

B. Complete each sentence with the correct form of the verb in ( ).

7. We _____ my sister to the farm. (take)

8. She _____ the brown cows. (admire)

9. They _____ under a big, leafy tree. (rest)

10. It _____ the cows cool. (keep)

11. You _____ the small pony in the red barn. (like)

12. He _____ an apple from my hand. (eat)

WRITE IT

Write sentences that compare country life and city life. Use pronouns and verbs in the present time. Write on a separate sheet of paper.

Using Pronouns and Verbs That Agree

Read each sentence pair. The subjects are underlined. Circle the present-time verbs.

1. <u>Kimi</u> wears big hats.   2. <u>The hats</u> flap in the wind.

   <u>She</u> wears big hats.   <u>They</u> flap in the wind.

 A verb in the present time must agree with the pronoun used in the subject of a sentence. Verbs used with <u>he</u>, <u>she</u>, or <u>it</u> end with <u>-s</u> or <u>-es</u>. Verbs used with <u>I</u>, <u>you</u>, <u>we</u>, and <u>they</u> do not end with <u>-s</u> or <u>-es</u>.

A. Complete the sentence with the correct form of the verb in ( ).

EXAMPLE: She _____builds_____ a table for our hats. (build, builds)

1. We _____ hats with feathers. (sell, sells)

2. They _____ the hats on the table. (see, sees)

3. She _____ the hat with the blue flower. (like, likes)

4. It _____ in the dark. (glow, glows)

5. He _____ the hat with a red band. (buy, buys)

6. You _____ a hat to Dad. (give, gives)

B. Write each sentence with the correct form of the verb in ( ).
EXAMPLE: He (see) a brown hat.
          <u>He sees a brown hat.</u>

7. He (wear) it proudly.

   _____

8. It (look) so fine on him.

   _____

9. We (buy) the handsome hat quickly.

   _____

Verbs in the Past

⊃ A verb in the **past time** shows action that already happened. Most verbs in the past time end in -ed.

A. Complete each sentence with a verb from the box. The word in ( ) tells you what kind of verb.

| traveled | talks | explored | covers | pulled |

1. Mrs. Cruz _____ about Richard Byrd. (present)

2. He _____ to Antarctica. (past)

3. A sheet of ice _____ most of the land. (present)

4. A team of dogs _____ sleds over the ice. (past)

5. Richard Byrd _____ the land there. (past)

B. Write the verb in ( ) in the past time. Write one letter on each line. Then use the circled letters to answer the question below.

6. The unusual birds (shock) him. __ __ __ ◯ __ __ __

7. He (enjoy) the playful birds. __ __ __ ◯ __ __ __

8. They (walk) quickly on the ice. __ __ ◯ __ __ __

9. The black and white feathers (look) like a suit. __ __ __ __ ◯

How does it feel in Antarctica? __ __ __ __

WRITE IT

On separate paper, write about an adventure you have had. Use verbs in the past time in your sentences.

© SILVER BURDETT GINN INC.

Verbs in the Past

Read the sentence. It uses a verb in the present time.

1. We paint the house.

Write the sentence. Make it tell about a past time.
Add -<u>ed</u> to the verb.

2. _____

 A verb in the **past time** shows action that already happened.
Most verbs in the past time end in -<u>ed</u>.

A. The verb is underlined in each sentence. Write each past-time verb
on a line below.
EXAMPLE: I <u>finished</u> the doghouse yesterday.

1. My friend Gary <u>helped</u> me with it.

2. We <u>hammered</u> nails along the edges.

3. Max <u>sits</u> proudly in his new house.

_____finished_____   _____   _____

B. Fill in each blank with the past-time form of the verb in ( ).
EXAMPLE: We _____washed_____ the car with soap. (wash)

4. Tina _____ the weeds in the garden. (pick)

5. She _____ the plants along the fence. (water)

6. Manuel _____ the dogs around the block. (walk)

7. I _____ the table and chairs. (dust)

8. They _____ the potatoes and carrots. (peel)

9. Shannon and I _____ the kitchen. (clean)

10. We _____ the refrigerator. (check)

11. Blackie _____ for his bones. (bark)

Grade 3, Unit 5, Lesson 4
GRAMMAR: Verbs in the Past Tense (Reteaching)

Spelling Verbs in the Present

⟩ Some verbs in the present time end in -s or -es. The spelling of some verbs changes when -es is added.

A. Complete each sentence with a verb from the picture. Write the form that ends with -s or -es.

1. The pitcher _____ low to the ground.

2. The player _____ the ball.

3. The ball _____ through the air.

fly

throw

pitch

B. Find the name of a baseball position. Complete each sentence with the verb in ( ). Write the form that ends in -s or -es on the blanks.

4. She _____ . (reach)   ____ ____ | ____ ____ ____

5. He _____ . (bat)   ____ ____ | ____ ____ ____

6. He _____ . (stretch)   ____ ____ | ____ ____ ____

7. She _____ . (catch)   ____ ____ | ____ ____ ____

8. It _____ . (hit)   ____ ____ | ____ ____ ____

9. He _____ . (leap)   ____ ____ | ____ ____ ____

10. It _____ . (roll)   ____ ____ | ____ ____ ____

WRITE IT

On separate paper, write sentences about a sport you like. Use verbs in the present time.

Spelling Verbs in the Present

Write each verb. Add the ending s.

1. walk _____walks_____   2. race _____

Write each verb. Add the ending es.

3. mix _____   4. wish _____

Write each verb. Change the y to i. Then add es.

5. dry _____   6. fry _____

➡ Some verbs in the present time end in -s or -es. Add -es to verbs that end in s, ss, x, ch, or sh. Change the y to i and add -es to verbs that end with a consonant and y.

A. Write each verb in the present time. Add -s or -es, or change the y to i and add -es. The first one is done for you.

1. fix _____fixes_____   4. hurry _____

2. eat _____   5. toss _____

3. rush _____   6. fly _____

B. Complete each sentence. Use the verb in ( ). Write the form that ends in -s or -es.

EXAMPLE: Yoko _____mixes_____ the corn batter. (mix)

7. She _____ it into a pan. (pour)

8. Her mom _____ the pan in the oven. (put)

9. Yoko _____ the batter rise. (watch)

10. She _____ the bread to the table. (take)

11. Her dad _____ the warm loaf. (cut)

12. He _____ for the butter. (search)

Spelling Verbs in the Past

Most verbs in the past time end in -ed. The spelling of some verbs changes when -ed is added.

A. Complete each sentence. Use the past-time of a verb in the box.

1. Sandy _____ to sing alone.

2. The class _____ their feet.

3. She _____ her hands.

4. We _____ our fingers.

5. Then Sandy _____ to rest.

| clap |
| snap |
| tap |
| stop |
| try |

B. Each underlined verb in the story is in the present time. Write each verb in the past time on a line.

> **WOODY SINGS FOR ALL!**
> APRIL 6, 1957 — The crowd <u>hurries</u> into the concert hall to hear the famous singer. The spotlight <u>dims</u>. Then onto the stage <u>steps</u> the singer, Woody Guthrie.
>
> Woody <u>likes</u> to sing songs about the beauty of America. The audience <u>listens</u> to Woody's guitar. His music <u>helps</u> us know the people around us.

6. _____

7. _____

8. _____

9. _____

10. _____

11. _____

WRITE IT

Write about a concert or show you have seen. Make sure you spell verbs in the past time correctly. Write on a separate sheet of paper.

Spelling Verbs in the Past

Circle the verb in each sentence.

1. Jennifer tossed her marker.   **2.** She hopped to the next box.

3. She tried her best today.

Did you notice that the spelling of <u>toss</u> does not change when <u>-ed</u> is added? The spellings of <u>hop</u> and <u>try</u> do change when <u>-ed</u> is added.

 Most verbs in the past time end in <u>-ed</u>. When a verb ends in a consonant and <u>y</u>, change <u>y</u> to <u>i</u> before adding <u>-ed</u>. When a verb ends in one vowel and one consonant, double the final consonant before adding <u>-ed</u>.

A. Complete each sentence. Write the past time of the verb in ( ).

EXAMPLE: Max _____studied_____ the game. (study)

1. He _____ his fingers on the table. (drum)

2. He _____ for a king. (wish)

3. Max _____ , "I see just the move!" (cry)

4. He _____ his piece over two red ones. (jump)

5. Sal then _____ over three. (skip)

6. They _____ the board home. (carry)

B. Complete each sentence. Use a word from the box. Write the correct verb in the past time.

EXAMPLE: Anita _____passed_____ the basketball.

7. Chloe almost _____ the ball.

8. She _____ for the back of the hoop.

9. The ball _____ through the hoop.

10. She _____ to catch the ball.

aim
hurry
drop
slip
pass

Prefixes

A. Complete each sentence. Add a prefix to each word in ( ).

1. Tao wants to _____ her snow house. (model)

2. She is _____ that it is melting. (happy)

3. Dad tells Tao to come in. She thinks it is _____ . (fair)

4. He will _____ the soup because it is cool. (heat)

B. Complete the puzzle. For each clue write a word that has the prefix re- or un-.

Down

5. opposite of fold

7. opposite of tie

8. opposite of kind

10. run again

11. use again

Across

6. paint again

8. opposite of important

9. do again

12. opposite of welcome

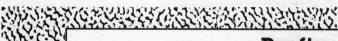

Prefixes

A **prefix** is a letter or letters added to the beginning of a word. A prefix changes the meaning of a word.

Read the chart below. Underline the prefix in each example word.

Prefix	Meaning	Examples
1. re-	again	retell, rebuild, reheat
2. un-	the opposite of	unfair, unable, unclear

A. Match each word to its meaning. The first one is done for you.

1. unneeded   marry again

2. renew   opposite of needed

3. unready   opposite of interesting

4. uninteresting   opposite of ready

5. remarry   make new again

B. Each word in the box has a prefix. Choose a word that means the same as the underlined words in each sentence. Write the word in the blank. The first one is done for you.

rewrite   unlike   retold   unknown   reread   unlucky

6. "Rumpelstiltskin" was written long ago by the Grimm brothers.

   It is <u>told again</u> by Edith Tarcov. _____retold_____

7. Eli will <u>read</u> the story <u>again</u> to his sister. _____

8. Mia wants to <u>write</u> her story <u>again</u>. _____

9. The hero of her story is <u>not lucky</u>. _____

10. The person who wrote that beautiful poem is <u>not known</u>.

    _____

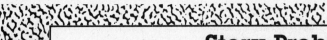

Story Problems

  In a story the main character has a problem to solve. The problem is solved by make-believe in a fairy tale.

A. Read each pair of sentences. Write <u>P</u> for each story problem. Write <u>S</u> for each solution.

1. The hero is trapped on an island. _____

   A friendly bird flies the hero to safety. _____

2. The hero turns the giant into a mouse. _____

   A hungry giant enters the town. _____

3. The key to the castle fell to the bottom of the sea. _____

   A fairy drew a picture of the key and it appeared. _____

B. Here are some story problems. Write a way to solve each one. You may use make-believe.

4. A dragon is burning all the forests in the kingdom.

   _____

5. The hero is sealed inside a cave.

   _____

6. The hero is lost at sea.

   _____

7. A princess is locked in a tower.

   _____

WRITE IT

Write about the story problem in a favorite fairy tale. Tell how the problem is solved. Write on a separate sheet of paper.

Story Problems

Match the words with the sentences.

1. Story Problem   A princess is lost in a forest.

2. Solution   A fairy shows the princess the way home.

 A story has a main character or hero. The main character has a problem to solve. The problem is solved by make-believe in a fairy tale.

A. Write <u>P</u> next to each story problem. You will find three problems.

EXAMPLE ___P___ A fairy is trapped inside a jar.

_____ **1.** The prince rescues the queen.

_____ **2.** The queen is surrounded by dragons.

_____ **3.** The princess lives happily ever after.

_____ **4.** The hero loses his magic sword.

_____ **5.** A giant is stealing food from the town.

B. Read each story problem. Draw a line to a possible solution. The first one is done for you.

Problem   **Solution**

6. The hero eats magic grapes. He falls into a deep sleep.

A fairy makes the dragon vanish.

7. A dragon roars angrily at the townspeople.

A princess says a magic word. The prince wakes.

8. A wind blows the queen's crown into the sky.

A bird flies after the crown and returns it to the queen.

Verbs with Special Past Forms

⊃ Some verbs in the past time do not end in -ed.

A. Circle each verb that shows past time. Write one verb in each car of the train.

came	run	went	ran	do
did	goes	had	comes	has

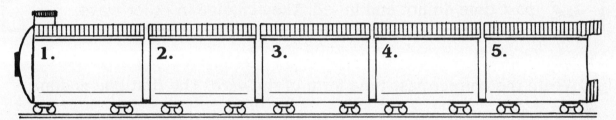

1. _____ 2. _____ 3. _____ 4. _____ 5. _____

B. Each underlined verb shows present time. Write the past-time form, one letter on each line.

6. Mr. Rose <u>runs</u> to catch the train.   ⊙ __ __

7. He <u>goes</u> down two flights of steps.   __ __ ⊙ __

8. Everyone <u>does</u> the same thing every day.   ⊙ __ __

9. The train <u>comes</u> into the station.   __ __ __ ⊙

10. Mr. Rose <u>runs</u> to the last car.   __ __ ⊙

11. The last car <u>has</u> an empty seat.   __ __ ⊙

C. Finish the sentence below. Write each circled letter above its sentence number.

12. The train traveled u ⊙ ⊙ ⊙ ⊙ the grou ⊙ ⊙ .
                   7 8 9 6   10 11

WRITE IT

Write sentences about a train ride. Use the past-time forms of the verbs <u>come</u>, <u>do</u>, <u>go</u>, <u>have</u>, and <u>run</u>. Write on a separate sheet of paper.

Verbs with Special Past Forms

Circle the past-time verb in each sentence. Use the chart to help you.	Present	Past	
	come, comes	came	
1. She went yesterday.	do, does	did	
	go, goes	went	
2. She came home early.	have, has	had	
	run, runs	ran	

 Most verbs in the past time end in <u>-ed</u>. Some verbs in the past time do not end in <u>-ed</u>. They change in other ways.

A. Write the correct past-time form of the verb. The first one is done for you.

1. come, comes _____came_____   3. do, does _____

2. go, goes _____   4. have, has _____

5. run, runs _____

B. Underline the past-time form of the verb in ( ). Then write the verb you underlined. The first one is done for you.

6. The children (go, <u>went</u>) to the pet show. _____went_____

7. Many parents (came, come) with them. _____

8. Some pets (did, do) tricks. _____

9. One dog (runs, ran) around a track. _____

10. A white cat (do, did) spins. _____

11. Each pet (goes, went) past the judges. _____

12. The judges (have, had) a hard time. _____

13. The ribbon (goes, went) to the snake. _____

14. Everyone (has, had) a good time. _____

The Verb *be*

A verb may show being. Use <u>am</u>, <u>is</u>, <u>are</u>, <u>was</u>, and <u>were</u> to tell what someone or something is or was.

A. Draw a line from the word <u>being</u> to each verb that shows being. Draw a line from the word <u>action</u> to each verb that shows action. Then write each verb.

1. _____   4. _____   6. _____   9. _____

2. _____   5. _____   7. _____   10. _____

3. _____   8. _____

B. Underline the verb in each sentence. Write the verbs that show being on the lines below.

11. Laura Ingalls Wilder was one of three daughters.

12. She lived in a little log cabin in Wisconsin.

13. Her family traveled by covered wagon.

14. Her stories are about American life in the 1870s.

15. I am a fan of Laura Ingalls Wilder.

16. _____   17. _____   18. _____

WRITE IT

Write sentences about an author or a book you like. Use the verbs <u>is</u>, <u>am</u>, <u>are</u>, <u>was</u>, and <u>were</u>. Write on a separate sheet of paper.

The Verb *be*

Read the sentences. The verbs are underlined.

José <u>is</u> a pitcher. He <u>throws</u> the ball.

1. Write the verb that shows action. _____

2. Write the verb that does not show action. _____

 A verb may show action. A verb also may show being. Use <u>am</u>, <u>is</u>, <u>are</u>, <u>was</u>, and <u>were</u> to tell what someone or something is or was.

A. Circle each verb that shows being. Write one verb in each bat.

play   were   was   run   are   catch   is   am

EXAMPLE: _____ were _____

1. _____   **3.** _____

2. _____   **4.** _____

B. Underline the verb in each sentence. If the verb shows being, write <u>being</u>. If the verb shows action, write <u>action</u>.

5. Alan <u>pitches</u> a fast ball. _____ action _____

6. The batter swings the bat. _____

7. The ball is over the fence. _____

8. There were three runners on base. _____

9. The coach is happy. _____

10. Their team wins the game. _____

Using the Forms of be

⟩ The form of <u>be</u> that is used must agree with the subject of
the sentence.

A. Draw a line from each sentence to a form of *be*. Use each verb in
the box. Then write the verb in the sentence. The first one is done
for you.

Verb Box

1. I _____ am _____ a guest on a farm.

2. We _____ guests on a farm.

3. Seven cows _____ in the pasture last week.

4. One cow _____ in the pasture yesterday.

5. A fence _____ around the pasture now.

6. Some fences _____ around the fields.

are
am
were
was
are
is

B. Complete each sentence. Write a word from the verb box above.
Then write each word in the puzzle.

Across

7. I _____ working on a farm.

8. Farms _____ once everywhere.

9. Today a farm _____ a big business.

Down

7. Many farms _____ in Wisconsin.

8. A farm of long ago _____ near our town.

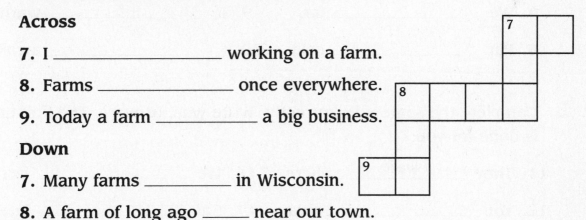

WRITE IT

Write about life on a farm. Use the verbs <u>am</u>, <u>is</u>, <u>are</u>, <u>was</u>, and
<u>were</u>. Write on a separate sheet of paper.

Using the Forms of be

Subject	Present	Past	Subject	Present	Past
I	am	was	you	are	were
he, she, it	is	was	we	are	were
singular noun	is	was	they	are	were
			plural noun	are	were

Look at the chart above. Circle the forms of <u>be</u> that repeat.

 When the correct subject and verb are used together, we say that they agree. The form of <u>be</u> that is used must agree with the subject of the sentence.

A. Complete the sentences correctly. Write <u>am</u>, <u>is</u>, or <u>are</u>. The first one is done for you.

1. They _____are_____ here.　　6. I _____ early.

2. You _____ there.　　7. Laura _____ away.

3. A dog _____ near.　　8. Cars _____ fast.

4. We _____ far.　　9. It _____ warm.

5. Pat _____ cold.　　10. I _____ awake.

B. Complete the sentences correctly. Write <u>was</u>, or <u>were</u>. The first one is done for you.

11. They _____were_____ here.　　16. We _____ far.

12. You _____ away.　　17. Sal _____ late.

13. Dogs _____ near.　　18. Ray _____ nice.

14. I _____ early.　　19. A car _____ there.

15. José _____ quick.　　20. They _____ fair.

Main Verbs and Helping Verbs

A **helping verb** works with the main verb. It helps to show action in the past time.

A. Complete each sentence with the correct form of a verb in the box.

| bake | gather | greet |

1. Everyone has _____ for Thanksgiving dinner.

2. Mother has _____ the guests.

3. People have _____ bread from corn flour.

B. Complete each sentence. Write a helping verb and the correct form of the main verb in ( ). Then answer the riddle below.

4. The Pilgrims __ __ __ __ __ __ __ __ __ __ for
$\quad$ $\overline{1}$ $\ \overline{6}$ $\quad \overline{3}$

days. (prepare)

5. They __ __ __ __ __ __ __ __ friends. (invite)
$\qquad \overline{7}$

6. They __ __ __ __ __ __ __ __ the meal. (enjoy)
$\qquad\qquad \overline{2}$

7. We __ __ __ __ __ __ __ __ __ __ to
$\qquad \overline{4} \ \overline{5}$

celebrate this day. (continue)

What did Squanto teach the Pilgrims to make? Look at the letters you wrote. Write the letters that have numbers.

$\dfrac{p}{1}$ $\ \overline{2}$ $\ \overline{3}$ $\ \overline{4}$ $\ \overline{5}$ $\ \overline{6}$ $\ \overline{7}$

WRITE IT

Describe how you helped on a special day. Use helping verbs in your sentences. Write on separate paper.

Main Verbs and Helping Verbs

The verb in each sentence is underlined. Circle the helping verbs <u>have</u>, <u>has</u>, and <u>had</u>.

1. The lion <u>has roared</u>.　　3. Dogs <u>have growled</u> nearby.

2. It <u>had roared</u> loudly.　　4. They <u>had growled</u> at the lion.

 A verb can be more than one word. A **helping verb** works with the main verb. It helps to show an action in the past.

A. Circle the helping verb and underline the main verb in each sentence.

Example: The skunk (has) spotted some danger.

1. Something strange had walked too close.

2. The skunk has lifted its front paws.

3. It has sprayed a smelly liquid.

4. Skunks have warned strangers this way often.

5. These strangers have leaped into the forest.

B. Complete each sentence with a helping verb. Use <u>has</u> after a singular subject. Use <u>have</u> after a plural subject.

Example: Some divers _____have_____ looked for the shark.

6. The shark _____ searched for food.

7. The seahorses _____ changed color to hide.

8. They _____ hidden from danger well.

9. One diver _____ watched the shark.

10. His eyes _____ followed every movement.

11. Several fish _____ stayed near the rocks.

12. The divers _____ admired their bright colors.

Using Irregular Verbs

➲ Some verbs change their form to show past time.

A. Underline the correct past-time verb in ( ).

1. The Samson family has (went, gone) on many trips.

2. They have (saw, seen) many cities.

3. They have (ate, eaten) all kinds of foods.

4. Last year Tina Samson (went, gone) on a long trip.

5. She (saw, seen) the Grand Canyon.

6. Tina (gave, given) me a picture of the canyon.

7. Last week Mike Samson (did, done) some planning.

8. Now he has (went, gone) to San Francisco.

B. Write the form of the verb in ( ) that correctly shows past time.

9. The Samsons have _____ to New York twice. (go)

10. They _____ their traveling by plane and bus. (do)

11. They have _____ the Statue of Liberty. (see)

12. Mike _____ me a model of it. (give)

13. The family _____ in the World Trade Center. (eat)

14. They _____ all of New York from its top. (see)

15. They had _____ lunch in Chinatown. (eat)

16. Then they _____ to a museum. (go)

17. They _____ huge dinosaur bones. (see)

WRITE IT

Write about a place you have visited. Include some irregular verbs in the past time. Write on separate paper.

Using Irregular Verbs

Verb	do	go	eat	give	see
Past	did	went	ate	gave	saw
Past with <u>have</u>, <u>has</u>, or <u>had</u>	done	gone	eaten	given	seen

Read each sentence. Then circle the past form of the verb <u>go</u> or <u>see</u>.

1. They <u>went</u> to the fair.   2. They <u>saw</u> many happy people.

⟳ Many verbs that show past time end in <u>-ed</u>. Some verbs change their form to show past time.

A. Write the correct past-time form of each underlined verb.

EXAMPLE: Carlos and Rita <u>eat</u> popcorn.   _____ate_____

1. Then they <u>do</u> something funny.   _____

2. They <u>go</u> to the Fun House of Mirrors.   _____

3. The mirrors <u>give</u> them quite a surprise.   _____

4. They <u>see</u> two tall and very thin people.   _____

B. Underline the correct past-time verb in ( ).
EXAMPLE: After Tina had (ate, <u>eaten</u>), she went on a ride.

5. She had (saw, seen) a shiny red car to drive.

6. She (gave, given) the wheel a sharp turn.

7. Crash! She (done, did) it!

8. Tina had (gone, went) into the next car.

9. The car had (done, did) no harm.

10. Tina and Sal finally (gone, went) home.

11. They (<u>ate</u>, eaten) some cool fruit.

Using Irregular Verbs

Irregular verbs have special past forms.

A. Underline the correct past-time verb in ( ).

1. President Lincoln (came, come) from a log cabin in Indiana.

2. His family had (knew, known) many hardships.

3. Lincoln (grew, grown) into a tall and serious man.

4. People (knew, known) him as a great speaker.

5. Lincoln (grew, grown) interested in government.

6. He (run, ran) for President in 1860.

7. Artists have (drew, drawn) many pictures of this great man.

B. Write the correct form of the verb in ( ).

8. President Jefferson _____ from Virginia. (past of <u>come</u>)

9. He _____ about farming and invented a special plow. (past of <u>know</u>)

10. He _____ plans for many buildings. (past of <u>draw</u>)

11. His writing _____ _____ great interest. (past of <u>draw</u> with <u>has</u>)

12. His words "All men are created equal" _____

    _____ familiar to Americans. (past of <u>grow</u> with <u>have</u>)

WRITE IT

Write sentences about another president of the United States. Use some irregular verbs from the lesson. Write on a separate sheet of paper.

Using Irregular Verbs

Verb	run	come	grow	know	draw
Past	ran	came	grew	knew	drew
Past with <u>have</u>, <u>has</u>, or <u>had</u>	run	come	grown	known	drawn

Read each sentence. Then circle the past form of the verb <u>know</u> or <u>run</u>.

1. They knew about the first basketball practice.
2. Players ran to the gymnasium.

 Irregular verbs have special past forms. They do not add <u>-ed</u> to show action in the past.

A. Write the correct past-time form of the verb in ( ).

EXAMPLE: Ella _____came_____ to the first basketball practice. (come)

1. Many team members had _____ very tall. (grow)

2. Ella _____ to the hoop. (run)

3. Ella _____ her next play. (know)

4. She had _____ down the court. (run)

B. Underline the correct past-time verb in ( ).

EXAMPLE: Ella's parents (<u>came</u>, come) to the final game.

5. The ball (came, come) to Ella.

6. Her winning shot (draw, drew) loud cheers.

7. Few people had (knew, known) about Ella's skill.

8. Ella's parents (ran, run) to her and hugged her.

9. They have (grew, grown) proud of her.

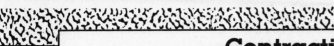

Contractions

 A **contraction** is a shortened form of two words. Some contractions are formed from a pronoun and a verb.

A. Write the correct contraction in place of the underlined words.

1. <u>I am</u> interested in alligators. _____

2. <u>I have</u> read books about them. _____

3. <u>We are</u> studying them in school. _____

4. <u>It is</u> true. Alligators have webbed feet. _____

5. <u>They are</u> found in warm waters. _____

6. <u>You will</u> see them in most zoos. _____

7. <u>I will</u> take you to see them. _____

B. Underline the contraction in each sentence. Then write the two words that make the contraction.

8. Today we'll meet Suzu Hama. _____

9. She's an expert on alligators. _____

10. I've talked to her twice. _____

11. She'll show us some alligators. _____

12. Perhaps we're in time for their feeding. _____

13. They're coming to the feeding pool now. _____

14. You'll see everything from here. _____

15. It's the best show at the zoo. _____

WRITE IT

On separate paper, write about a zoo animal that interests you. Use contractions in your sentences.

Contractions

One sentence uses a contraction. That sentence is shorter. Check (✓) the sentence that uses the contraction for <u>we will</u>.

1. We will go to the circus today with Tom. ☐

2. We'll go to the circus today with Tom. ☐

 A **contraction** is a shortened form of two words. Some contractions are formed from a pronoun and a verb. An apostrophe (') shows where a letter or letters are left out.

A. Circle the sentence in each pair that has a contraction. The first one is done for you.

1. (You'll have a great time at the circus.) It is so much fun.

2. It is the largest circus ever. I'm so excited.

3. I'll buy peanuts and popcorn. You will share them with me.

4. We will laugh at the clowns. They're always funny.

5. The elephant will do tricks. He's very large.

B. Write the contraction for the underlined words. The first one is done for you.

6. <u>It is</u> time for the circus to start. _____It's_____

7. I know <u>you will</u> love the dancing horses. _____

8. <u>I have</u> never been to a three-ring circus. _____

9. Now <u>I am</u> watching the bears perform. _____

10. <u>They are</u> riding on bicycles. _____

11. <u>You have</u> seen the last act. _____

12. <u>We will</u> return next year. _____

13. Now <u>we are</u> going home. _____

Suffixes

A. Read each sentence below. Choose a word from the box to complete each sentence. Write the word in the blank.

sailor	singer	reporter	player
traveler	reader	climber	

1. Someone who reports is a _____ .

2. Someone who sings is a _____ .

3. Someone who travels is a _____ .

4. Someone who plays is a _____ .

5. Someone who reads is a _____ .

6. Someone who sails is a _____ .

7. Someone who climbs is a _____ .

B. Add the suffix in ( ) to a word in the first sentence. Write the new word in the blank.

8. George likes to invent new things.

   He is an _____ . (-or)

9. Marta will work hard on the class project.

   She is a hard _____ . (-er)

10. Mr. Rivera will build his own house.

    He is a _____ . (-er)

11. Taro likes to photograph his family.

    He is a good _____ . (-er)

12. Cara will direct the class play.

    She will be the _____ . (-or)

Suffixes

A letter or letters added to the end of a word is a **suffix**. The suffixes -er or -or mean "someone who."

Read the first sentence. Complete the second sentence by adding a suffix to the underlined word.

1. Mr. Chin likes to <u>teach</u>. He is a _____ .

2. Ms. Akoni will <u>visit</u> us. She is a _____ .

A. Write the word that describes each person. The first one is done for you.

| catcher   painter   trainer   conductor   farmer   sweeper |

1.

2.

3.

<u>conductor</u> _____   _____   _____

4.

5.

6.

_____   _____   _____

B. Complete the puzzle. The filled-in letter helps you know if the suffix is -<u>er</u> or -<u>or</u>. The first one is done for you.

7. someone who plants   <u>p</u> <u>l</u> <u>a</u> <u>n</u> <u>t</u> <u>e</u> <u>r</u>

8. someone who thinks   ___ ___ ___ ___ ___ <u>e</u> ___

9. someone who acts   ___ ___ ___ <u>o</u> ___

NAME _____

Choosing a Topic

> Choose a topic that interests you. If the topic is too broad, you must narrow it down.

A. Put an X over each topic that is broad.

1. the nine planets
2. robins
3. famous football players
4. Mark Twain's childhood
5. authors
6. cooking

7. the first airplane flight
8. great rivers of the world
9. the history of the United States
10. how to paint a picture
11. goldfish
12. plants

B. Choose a narrow topic from the words in the box. Write the narrow topic next to the broad one.

Broad   **Narrow**

13. animal _____
14. clothes _____
15. home _____
16. food _____
17. tree _____
18. metal _____
19. games _____

| bread |
| tag |
| fox |
| hive |
| iron |
| hat |
| oak |

WRITE IT

Write a narrower topic for each broad one. Write on a separate sheet of paper.

famous women   the history of cars   zoo animals

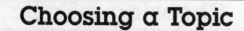

Choosing a Topic

Read each sentence. Answer each question about writing a report.

1. Amy wants to write about sports. Can she tell about them all

   in a short report? _____ Yes   _____ No

2. Mika wants to write a report about Babe Ruth. Can she tell about

   him in a short report? _____ Yes   _____ No

 Choose a topic that interests you. If the topic is too broad, you must narrow it down.

A. Write the narrower topic in each pair.

EXAMPLE: American cities, Houston _____ Houston _____

1. roses, flowers _____

2. grasshoppers, insects _____

3. musical instruments, drums _____

4. zoos, the Bronx Zoo _____

5. the human body, eyes _____

6. Jimmy Carter, Presidents _____

B. Draw a line from each broad topic to its narrow topic. The first one is done for you.

Broad	Narrow
7. sports stars	how to care for a cat
8. how to make birthday gifts	the first king of Spain
9. caring for pets	Don Mattingly
10. the southern states	making a bead necklace
11. the history of Spain	Georgia

Using the Library

> A library has many kinds of books. Books of the same kind are grouped together.

A. Write each book title under the correct heading.

The Life of George Washington   Making Model Airplanes

Dumbo   Dictionary for Children

Mystery at Big Bluff   Encyclopedia Britannica

Fiction	Nonfiction
1. _____	3. _____
2. _____	4. _____

Reference

5. _____   6. _____

B. Tell which kind of book would have each kind of information. Write <u>biography</u>, <u>atlas</u>, <u>dictionary</u>, or <u>encyclopedia</u>.

7. two meanings for the word <u>odd</u>   _____

8. maps of Mexico and Canada   _____

9. information about bees, Thomas
   Edison, and Texas   _____

10. the complete life story of Thomas
    Edison   _____

11. information about trucking   _____

WRITE IT

List the titles of five books you know. Next to each title, tell whether the book is <u>fiction</u>, <u>nonfiction</u>, or <u>reference</u>. Write on a separate sheet of paper.

Using the Library

Read each sentence. Underline the word in each sentence that tells the kind of book described.

1. A **fiction** book tells a made-up story.

2. A **nonfiction** book tells about the real world.

3. A **reference** book gives information about many subjects.

 A library has fiction, nonfiction, and reference books. Books of the same kind are grouped together.

A. Read about the books below. Draw a line to the kind each is. The first one is done for you.

1. a set of books telling about many subjects

2. the life of Jesse Jackson

3. a book of maps

4. the story of Cinderella

5. a book about fish

6. the story of a talking bus

| fiction |

| nonfiction |

| reference |

B. Read each book title. Write <u>fiction</u>, <u>nonfiction</u>, or <u>reference</u> for each one.

EXAMPLE: <u>The Tale of Peter Rabbit</u>   fiction

7. <u>Compton's Encyclopedia</u>   _____

8. <u>The Big Book of Trains</u>   _____

9. <u>The Life of Pocahontas</u>   _____

10. <u>How the Grinch Stole Christmas</u>   _____

11. <u>Webster's Dictionary</u>   _____

Taking Notes in Your Own Words

To help you remember information you read, take notes in your own words. Write just enough to help you remember.

A. Read each sentence about fire. Choose the better note for each sentence. Write it in the blank.

1. Fire has many uses.
   a. fire—many uses
   b. fire
   _____

2. People use fire to keep warm.
   a. people use
   b. to keep warm
   _____

3. Hot fires can melt metal.
   a. fires can melt
   b. melt metal
   _____

4. People shape the hot metal into tools.
   a. shaping metal tools
   b. shaping metal
   _____

B. Read the paragraph below. Then use your own words to write about what you learned.

Early peoples made fire by rubbing pieces of wood together. Fire kept them warm and dry. They used fire to keep wild animals away. They cooked over fires. They also hardened clay pots inside fires.

_____

_____

WRITE IT

Read a paragraph in your science book. On a separate sheet of paper, take notes in your own words.

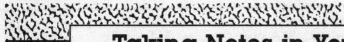

Taking Notes in Your Own Words

Two boys read the sentence below. Then they wrote notes. Circle the note that would help you remember the sentence best.

All insects have six legs.

1. insects—six legs   2. six

 To help you remember information you read, take notes in your own words. Write just enough to help you remember.

A. Read the sentences about insects and the notes. Circle the better note for each sentence.

EXAMPLE: An insect's body has three parts.
a. insect body   **b.** body—three parts

1. All insects have three pairs of legs.

    a. 3 pairs of legs   **b.** three pairs

2. Many have eyes made up of many tinier eyes.

    a. eyes with tinier eyes   **b.** insects—tinier eyes

3. Most insects are land animals.

    a. most—land animals   **b.** most—animals

4. Many live in the fresh water of lakes and streams.

    a. lakes and streams   **b.** many—lakes, streams

5. Few insects live in salt water.

    a. few—salt water   **b.** few—salt

B. Read the paragraph. Write notes in your own words.

The firefly is a kind of beetle. It is sometimes called the "lightning bug." This insect can turn its glow off and on.

_____

_____

Writing with Adjectives

⊃ A word that describes a noun is an **adjective**.

A. Write in each sentence an adjective from the box. The sentence must make sense. Use each adjective once.

fancy	white	long	soft	wonderful	large

1. Some _____ webs brushed my face.

2. I looked inside a _____ trunk.

3. The trunk was filled with _____ clothes.

4. I discovered a _____ cape.

5. I also found a _____ dress.

6. I had a _____ morning in the attic.

B. Complete each sentence by adding an adjective.

7. It was a _____ day.

8. I explored our _____ attic.

9. I climbed the _____ stairs.

10. I opened the _____ door.

11. The room was filled with _____ furniture.

12. A _____ moth flew by.

WRITE IT

On separate paper, list things you might find in an attic. Use an adjective to describe each one.

Writing with Adjectives

The words below may be used to describe nouns. Circle the words that best describe the nouns <u>snow</u>, <u>ball</u>, <u>lemon</u>, <u>lion</u>, and <u>fire</u>.

   rusty      salty   smoky

          white   sour   fresh

   hard   loud

          flat   quiet

 A word that describes a noun is an **adjective.** An adjective may tell how something looks, feels, tastes, smells, or sounds.

A. A noun is underlined in each sentence. Circle the adjective that tells how that noun looks, feels, tastes, smells, or sounds.

EXAMPLE: (White) <u>clouds</u> float in the sky.

1. A girl walked along the quiet <u>beach</u>.

2. The soft <u>sand</u> tickled her feet.

3. She sniffed the fresh <u>air</u>.

4. A pail lay on the clean <u>beach</u>.

5. Noisy <u>crowds</u> play in the shade.

B. Complete each sentence with an adjective.

EXAMPLE: A _____small_____ boy plays with a pail.

5. He fills it with _____ shells.

6. _____ flowers grow on the hill.

7. _____ sunshine fills the day.

8. She bites the _____ peach.

9. Fish swim in the _____ water.

Adjectives That Tell *How Many*

⊃ Some adjectives answer the question "How many?"

A. Write each adjective that tells <u>how many</u>.

1. We ride in one small car. _____

2. We have four large bags. _____

3. My two puppies sit with me. _____

4. We see many cars at the airport. _____

5. We watch several planes. _____

B. Circle in the puzzle the six adjectives that tell how many. Then write one adjective in each sentence.

```
r  s  t  s  o  m  e
a  e  b  n  n  d  g
w  v  f  i  r  f  m
t  e  n  n  n  g  o
a  r  c  e  e  w  l
p  a  b  t  o  n  e
r  l  s  y  t  w  o
```

6. Our trip took _____ hours.

7. The plane carried _____ people.

8. We ate _____ meal.

9. The plane made _____ stops.

10. _____ people got on.

11. The plane arrived _____ minutes early.

WRITE IT

Describe something you like to ride on. Use adjectives that tell <u>how many</u>. Write on a separate sheet of paper.

Adjectives That Tell *How Many*

six	some
several	four
two	many

Look at this funny machine. Then write one word to complete each sentence. Choose a word from the box.

1. I see _____ wheels spinning.

2. I see _____ bottles traveling.

The words you wrote are adjectives. They describe the nouns <u>wheels</u> and <u>bottles</u>. They answer the question "How many?"

 Some adjectives answer the question "How many?" They may be exact numbers such as <u>six</u> and <u>four</u>. They may be words such as <u>some</u> and <u>many</u>.

A. Circle each adjective that answers the question "How many?" The first one is done for you.

1. She saw (two) turtles.

2. They saw six skunks.

3. He smelled four flowers.

4. We heard many monkeys.

5. I tasted five figs.

6. She heard three thumps.

7. I felt some stones.

8. They saw several seals.

B. Complete each sentence. Write the adjective that tells <u>how many</u>.

EXAMPLE: They smelled a _____*few*_____ roses. (red, few)

9. We saw _____ toads. (ten, green)

10. He tasted _____ mushrooms. (soft, many)

11. They heard _____ flutes. (sweet, fifteen)

12. We tasted _____ sandwiches. (several, thick)

Adjectives That Tell *What Kind*

> Some adjectives answer the question "What kind?"

A. Circle the two adjectives in each sentence that tell <u>what kind</u>. Then write them.

1. Lani unrolled the long green hose.

   _____ _____

2. We opened the low white gate.

   _____ _____

3. Tall colorful flowers grew in our garden.

   _____ _____

4. A tiny playful chipmunk stood near the roses.

   _____ _____

B. Write an adjective that tells <u>what kind</u> to complete each sentence.

5. Lani raked the _____ soil.

6. It was a _____ morning.

7. We planted _____ seeds.

8. We put them in _____ rows.

9. We picked _____ tomatoes in August.

WRITE IT

Write about a garden you might like to plant. Use adjectives that tell <u>what kind</u>. Write on a separate sheet of paper.

Adjectives That Tell *What Kind*

Look at the picture of oranges. Write adjectives that describe oranges.

   1. _____   2. _____   3. _____

Did you use words such as *round, firm, orange, juicy,* and *delicious?* These words are adjectives that answer the question "What kind?"

 Some adjectives answer the question "What kind?" Adjectives may tell about size, shape, or color. They tell how things look, sound, feel, taste, or smell.

A. Draw a line to the adjective that best tells <u>what kind</u>.

    EXAMPLE: string bean   sweet

             honey   long

1. box   yellow

2. banana   salty

3. pin   square

4. ocean   tiny

B. All the adjectives tell <u>what kind</u>. Write the two adjectives that best describe each noun.

    EXAMPLE: _____crisp_____ _____green_____ lettuce
            (crisp, green, blue)

5. _____ , _____ grapes (small, square, juicy)

6. _____ _____ bread (fresh, curly, wheat)

7. _____ , _____ ice (hot, cold, shiny)

8. _____ , _____ peach (soft, six, fuzzy)

Using Adjectives That Compare

Use the -er form of an adjective to compare two persons, places, or things. Use the -est form of an adjective to compare three or more persons, places, or things.

A. Underline the correct adjective in ( ). Write it in the blank.

1. Anna is the (younger, youngest) one in her family. _____

2. Mia is (older, oldest) than her brother. _____

3. Ricky is (taller, tallest) than his dad. _____

4. Grandpa's eyes are (darker, darkest) than Grandma's. _____

5. Grandpa is the (calmer, calmest) person I know. _____

6. Tony is the (nicer, nicest) of all. _____

B. Complete each sentence. Write the correct -er or -est form of the adjective in ( ).

7. Maria is _____ than her brother. (short)

8. Carlos jumps _____ than Maria. (high)

9. Rosa is the _____ one of all. (small)

10. Maria has the _____ hair in the whole family. (long)

11. Her hair is _____ than Diane's. (straight)

WRITE IT

Write about fast or slow things, such as cars, insects, or animals. Use adjectives that compare in your sentences. Write on a separate sheet of paper.

Using Adjectives That Compare

Study the picture. Then complete each sentence.

1. _____ is stronger than Malcomb.

2. _____ is the strongest of all.

Did you notice that the word
<u>stronger</u> compared two people? Did
you notice that the word <u>strongest</u>
compared three people?

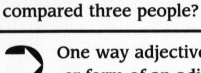

Paul   **José**

Malcomb

One way adjectives describe nouns is by comparing. Use the
<u>-er</u> form of an adjective to compare two persons, places, or
things. Use the <u>-est</u> form to compare three or more persons,
places, or things.

A. Write the <u>-er</u> and <u>-est</u> forms of each adjective.

EXAMPLE: slow _____slower_____   _____slowest_____

1. warm   _____   _____

2. sharp   _____   _____

3. quick   _____   _____

4. great   _____   _____

B. Circle the correct adjective in ( ). Then write it in the blank.

EXAMPLE: A tree is _____higher_____ than a bush. ((higher)
highest)

5. A lake is _____ than a pond. (wider, widest)

6. She is the _____ runner of all. (faster, fastest)

7. It is the _____ day of the year. (colder, coldest)

8. He is the _____ boy in class. (older, oldest)

Using a, an, and the

> The words <u>a</u>, <u>an</u>, and <u>the</u> are a special kind of adjective. They are called **articles**.

A. Complete each sentence. Write the correct article in ( ).

1. A honeybee is _____ insect. (a, an)

2. It is _____ busy worker, too. (a, an)

3. First it gathers sweet juice from _____ flowers. (the, a)

4. Then it carries it back to _____ hive. (an, the)

5. There _____ juice changes to honey! (the, a)

6. Honey is _____ delicious food. (a, an)

B. Unscramble the answers in ( ) and write them on the lines. Then circle the correct article in each sentence.

7. Have you ever slept on (ⓐ, an) feather pillow?

8. The feathers come from (a, an) _____ .   (c u d k)

9. Have you ever worn (a, an) scarf made of wool?

10. Wool comes from (a, an) _____ .   (p h e e s)

11. Would you like (a, an) icy cold glass of milk?

12. Milk comes from (a, an) _____ .   (w o c)

13. Do you like (a, an) egg salad?

14. Eggs come from (a, an) _____ .   (e n h)

WRITE IT

Write about your favorite meal. Use articles correctly in your sentences. Write on a separate sheet of paper.

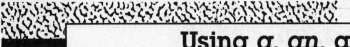

Using a, an, and the

Read the word groups below. Circle the words <u>a</u>, <u>an</u>, and <u>the</u> in each group. Check (✓) the things you would like to find in your lunch box.

____ an orange   ____ the sandwich   ____ a roll

____ an egg   ____ a carrot   ____ the cheese

The words <u>a</u>, <u>an</u>, and <u>the</u> are a special kind of adjective. They are called **articles.** <u>The</u> is used before singular and plural nouns. <u>A</u> is used with singular nouns that begin with a consonant sound. <u>An</u> is used before singular nouns that begin with a vowel sound.

A. Choose <u>a</u> or <u>an</u> for each word group. Write it in the blank.

EXAMPLE ___an___ uncooked potato

1. _____ delicious snack   5. _____ icy glass

2. _____ empty box of rice   6. _____ old cup

3. _____ large pickle   7. _____ loaf of bread

4. _____ can of peaches   8. _____ onion skin

B. Complete each sentence. Circle the correct article in ( ).
EXAMPLE: You can make ((a,) an) good drink from lemons.

9. Lemonade is (a, an) easy drink to make.

10. Squeeze (an, the) big yellow lemons.

11. Pour the juice into (a, an) big jar.

12. Add water to (the, an) jar.

13. Drink the lemonade outside under (a, an) umbrella.

14. Enjoy (an, the) cool drink.

Synonyms

A. For each word in dark print, circle two synonyms.

1. **pretty**: beautiful   neat   ugly   lovely

2. **same**: different   alike   equal   changed

3. **cold**: warm   cool   pleasant   icy

4. **awful**: bad   nice   terrible   okay

5. **bright**: old   dull   glowing   shining

6. **like**: love   enjoy   hate   unkind

7. **big**: small   large   huge   short

8. **laugh**: talk   chuckle   whisper   giggle

9. **small**: large   little   tiny   tall

B. Rewrite each sentence. Use a synonym for the underlined word.

10. Leaves turn pretty colors in the <u>autumn</u>.

_____

11. Dad said our room was very <u>neat</u>!

_____

12. Nicole will <u>remain</u> to put the leaves in bags.

_____

13. After working, Nicole is <u>sleepy</u>.

_____

14. She closes her eyes and takes a <u>rest</u>.

_____

15. After her rest, she is ready for <u>supper</u>.

_____

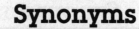

Synonyms

Synonyms are words that have almost the same meaning. Complete the last sentence with a synonym for the underlined words.

Mr. Kwan is a <u>pleasant</u> teacher.

Mr. Kwan is a <u>kind</u> teacher.

Mr. Kwan is a _____ teacher.

A. Match each word to its synonym. The first one is done for you.

1. smart	gloomy	5. cheerful	clean
2. fast	wise	6. neat	start
3. dark	quick	7. same	happy
4. small	little	8. begin	alike

B. Rewrite each sentence. Choose a word from the box to replace each underlined word.

help   like   tasty   quiet   sad   hot

EXAMPLE: Mom is <u>unhappy</u> that she cannot attend the circus.

Mom is sad that she cannot attend the circus.

9. Someone will <u>aid</u> you if you cannot find your seat.

_____

10. Everyone is <u>silent</u> as the lights are dimmed.

_____

11. The clowns look <u>warm</u> in their costumes.

_____

12. After the show we will have a <u>delicious</u> snack.

_____

Using Your Senses to Describe

Writers describe what they see, hear, taste, smell, and touch.

A. Write a word to describe each thing below. Use a different word each time.

1. the way mud feels between your toes _____

2. how pudding tastes _____

3. the smells in the kitchen _____

4. how a sack of potatoes feels _____

5. how an ear of corn tastes _____

B. Write a sentence that describes each thing below.

6. the way snow feels on your face

_____

7. the smell of wood burning in a fireplace

_____

8. the taste of pumpkin pie

_____

9. the way rocks feel when you walk on them.

_____

10. the way watermelon feels in your mouth

_____

WRITE IT

Imagine that you are enjoying a holiday dinner. Write sentences that use words to tell how the dinner tastes, smells, and feels. Write on a separate sheet of paper.

Using Your Senses to Describe

Tell how an orange tastes, smells, and feels. Write your words on the lines below.

taste _____

smell _____

feel _____

Writers describe what they see, hear, taste, smell, and touch. When you write a description, use your senses to tell details that describe.

A. Decide whether the words below tell how something tastes, smells, or feels. Write taste, smell, or feel.

EXAMPLE: soft _____feel_____

1. lumpy _____   4. rough _____

2. rotten _____   5. dry _____

3. spicy _____   6. salty _____

B. Write the word from the box that best describes each object.

| sticky smoky sharp sour |
| scratchy smooth sweet spicy salty |

EXAMPLE: glass _____smooth_____

7. lemon _____   11. glue _____

8. fire _____   12. popcorn _____

9. scissors _____   13. flowers _____

10. beard _____   14. pepper _____

A Paragraph That Describes

A **paragraph** can give a description. Begin with a topic sentence that tells the main idea. Then give details about the topic sentence.

A. Read the topic sentence in dark type. Write six sentences that give details about it.

In the winter, my family gathers in front of our fireplace.

1. _____

2. _____

3. _____

4. _____

5. _____

6. _____

B. Complete the topic sentence below with one of the following words: <u>fall</u>, <u>winter</u>, spring, <u>summer</u>. Then write detail sentences describing what you see, hear, smell, taste, or touch during that season.

My favorite season is _____

_____

_____

_____

WRITE IT

Write a paragraph about your favorite outdoor place. First, write a topic sentence about the place you choose. Then write four detail sentences that describe it. Write on a separate sheet of paper.

A Paragraph That Describes

Peng began his paragraph with this topic sentence: My garden is a busy place. The topic sentence states the main idea. Underline three sentences below that tell details about the main idea.

1. A frog hops in the damp grass.   3. A girl slips on the icy pond.
2. The crickets chirp summer songs. 4. A squirrel digs the soft earth.

Now complete the paragraph below. Write the sentences you underlined that describe Peng's busy garden.

My garden is a busy place. _____

_____

_____

 A paragraph can give a description. Begin with a topic sentence that tells the main idea. Then give details about the topic sentence. Paint a picture in words for your reader.

A. Read this paragraph. Draw one line under the topic sentence. Draw two lines under each detail sentence. One detail sentence is done for you.

The apple tree in my yard reminded me of my childhood. <u>Every year the fresh green buds told me it was spring.</u> Soon the sweet smell of the flowers swept through the windows. When we bit into the delicious red apples, there was a chill in the air.

B. Read the topic sentence in dark type. Draw a line under each detail sentence that tells about the topic sentence.

Peng likes to eat the vegetables from his garden.

1. He enjoys the juicy red tomatoes best.

2. He likes the crunchy beans, too.

3. The bees like the garden.

4. The crisp green peppers are sweet.

NAME _____

Nouns in Sentences

The main word in the subject of a sentence is often a noun.

A. The subject is underlined in each sentence. Circle the main word.

1. Some <u>fish</u> swim in a big tank.

2. A tall <u>boy</u> watches them.

3. Two <u>parrots</u> chatter loudly.

4. Three yellow <u>canaries</u> sing the same song.

5. A small <u>kitten</u> meows softly.

6. <u>The store</u> has many good pets for children.

B. The main word in each subject is underlined. Change this noun to a different noun. Write a new sentence.

7. Four <u>puppies</u> play in the store window.

   _____

8. Many <u>people</u> look at them.

   _____

9. Two <u>girls</u> walk into the pet store.

   _____

10. A small <u>kitten</u> sleeps in a corner.

    _____

11. A <u>rabbit</u> nibbles its food.

    _____

WRITE IT

Write about a pet store. Then circle the main word in each subject. Write on a separate sheet of paper.

Nouns in Sentences

A line is drawn after the subject part of each sentence. Complete each subject with a word from the box.

| logs |
| boats |
| children |
| tires |

1. The _____ | float in the lake.

2. Two happy _____ | float in the lake.

 The subject of a sentence names someone or something. The main word in the subject of a sentence often is a noun.

A. The subject is underlined in each sentence. Circle the main word in each subject.

EXAMPLE: Several (people) walk along the dock.

1. Many boats are tied there.

2. A woman hops into a small boat.

3. A boy unties the knot.

4. White sails go up.

5. The wind pushes the sails.

6. Some puffy clouds float in the sky.

B. Complete each subject with a noun. Write a noun from the box.

| day   sail   people   sailor   ducks |

EXAMPLE: The _____ sail _____ flaps in the wind.

7. The _____ is warm and sunny.

8. A _____ steers the boat.

9. Some _____ quack behind the boat.

10. A few _____ watch from the dock.

Verbs in Sentences

⟳ The main word in the predicate of a sentence is a verb. Every sentence needs to have a verb in the predicate.

A. The predicate part in each sentence is underlined. Circle the verb.

1. The farmer <u>plants rows of bushes.</u>

2. Berries <u>grow on the low bushes.</u>

3. Sun and water <u>help them grow.</u>

4. Some workers <u>pick the ripe juicy berries.</u>

5. Their alarm clocks <u>wake them at six o'clock.</u>

6. They <u>work in the early morning.</u>

B. Complete each predicate with a verb. Use a verb from the box. The first one is done for you.

sniffs washes drives loads invites eats bakes buys

7. A worker _____loads_____ the berries on a truck.

8. The truck _____ them to the market.

9. Dad _____ several boxes there.

10. Mom _____ them in the sink.

11. My sister _____ some bread in the oven.

12. Mr. Beard _____ a wonderful smell.

13. Dad _____ him for a snack.

14. My brother _____ three big pieces.

WRITE IT

On separate paper, write about something you have cooked. Be sure to use verbs that express action.

Verbs in Sentences

One word is missing from each sentence. It is the main word in the predicate. Write a verb to complete each one.

1. Three cows _____ in the meadow.

2. Some people _____ them closely.

The main word in a predicate is a verb. Every sentence needs to have a verb in the predicate. The predicate tells what the subject is or does.

A. The predicate is underlined in each sentence. Circle the verb in each predicate.

EXAMPLE: Two artists (drive) to the country.

1. They take paints and brushes with them.

2. They stop near the grassy meadow.

3. Four bluebirds rest in the tall soft grass.

4. Yellow flowers grow under their feet.

5. Some squirrels jump into an oak tree.

6. The women talk in soft voices.

B. Write a verb in the predicate of each sentence. Use a word from the box. The first one is done for you.

opens	paints	carries	sparkles	puts

7. Debra _____ carries _____ a cloth bag of paints.

8. She _____ a tube of green paint.

9. She _____ some on a long, thin brush.

10. She _____ the gentle green meadow.

11. The wet grass _____ in the sunlight.

Writing with Adverbs

⟩ A word that describes a verb is an **adverb**.

A. Find the adverb in each sentence. Underline it if it tells <u>where</u>. Circle it if it tells <u>when</u>.

1. The people leave the harbor early.

2. Large fishing boats take them out.

3. The boats travel far.

4. They always carry big nets with them.

5. They drop the big nets down.

6. The crew will fish there.

B. Complete each sentence with an adverb that answers the question in ( ).

7. The boats return to the harbor _____ . (When?)

8. They _____ bring many big fish with them. (When?)

9. Sometimes the crew catch many fish _____ . (Where?)

10. _____ the crew saw a whale! (When?)

11. _____ many people gather. (When?)

12. They buy fresh fish _____ . (Where?)

13. People _____ like fish for dinner. (Where?)

WRITE IT

On separate paper, write sentences about the ocean. Try to use adverbs that tell <u>where</u> and <u>when</u>.

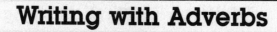

Writing with Adverbs

Read each sentence. The arrows show that <u>often</u> and <u>here</u> describe a verb. Underline each verb.

1. Children play often.   2. They play here.

 A word that describes a verb is an **adverb.** Adverbs may tell <u>when</u> an action happens. Adverbs may tell <u>where</u> an action happens.

A Write whether the underlined adverb tells <u>where</u> or <u>when</u>.

EXAMPLE: <u>Yesterday</u> the class made costumes.   _____when_____

1. They will practice the play <u>tomorrow</u>.   _____

2. <u>Now</u> they paint a big sign.   _____

3. They will hang the sign <u>outside</u>.   _____

4. The tickets are sold <u>inside</u>.   _____

5. Some people bought ten tickets <u>today</u>.   _____

B. Each verb that shows action is underlined. Circle the adverb that tells <u>where</u> or <u>when</u>. Write it in the blank.

EXAMPLE: Many people <u>arrive</u> (early.)   _____early_____

6. They <u>walk</u> upstairs.   _____

7. Some young children <u>run</u> around.   _____

8. The play <u>begins</u> soon.   _____

9. The audience <u>sits</u> down.   _____

10. The heavy red curtain <u>goes</u> up.   _____

11. The play <u>ends</u> late.   _____

12. People <u>clap</u> often.   _____

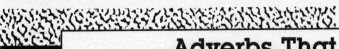

Adverbs That Tell *How*

⟩ Some adverbs answer the question "How?" Many adverbs that answer the question "How?" end in <u>-ly</u>.

A. Circle the adverb in each sentence. Then write it in the blank.

1. Glenn cheerfully whistled a tune. _____

2. He quickly sanded the new fence. _____

3. José mixed the red paint neatly. _____

4. The boys painted the boards of _____
   the fence evenly.

5. "Thank you boys," Dad smiled _____
   brightly.

B. Add <u>-ly</u> to each word in ( ) to form an adverb. Write the adverb in the sentence.

6. The clock in the kitchen _____ stopped.
   (sudden)

7. Betsy opened the back _____ . (slow)

8. She examined the clock parts _____ .
   (close)

9. She _____ cleaned the wheels of the
   clock. (careful)

10. The clock works _____ . (perfect)

11. "I fixed it!" Betsy exclaims _____ .
    (proud)

WRITE IT

On separate paper, write about something you have fixed. Use adverbs that answer the question "How?"

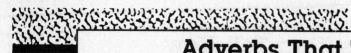

Adverbs That Tell *How*

Complete the sentences. Add -ly to the word quick.

1. Ana runs _____ to the finish line.

2. She _____ wins the race.

 A word that describes a verb is an **adverb.** Some adverbs answer the question "How?" Many adverbs that answer the question "How?" end in -ly.

A. Circle the adverb in each sentence. Then write it in the blank.

EXAMPLE: The children silently look. _____silently_____

1. Max suddenly notices marks in the sand. _____

2. Rosa examines them curiously. _____

3. "They are a rabbit's footprints!" she says wisely. _____

4. Max and Rosa follow the footprints eagerly. _____

B. Complete each sentence. Add -ly to each word in ( ) to form an adverb.

EXAMPLE: A turtle moves _____slowly_____ . (slow)

5. A fox dashes _____ . (swift)

6. A crow calls _____ . (loud)

7. The bird sings _____ . (sweet)

8. The cubs jump _____ . (playful)

9. A deer _____ looks for apples. (careful)

Contractions

⊃ Some contractions are formed from a verb and <u>not</u>.

A. Write the two words that make each contraction.

1. aren't _____ _____   5. doesn't _____ _____

2. weren't _____ _____   6. haven't _____ _____

3. shouldn't _____ _____   7. won't _____ _____

4. don't _____ _____   8. wouldn't _____ _____

B. Write a contraction to replace the underlined words.

9. The telephone <u>is not</u> working today. _____

10. It <u>does not</u> ring. _____

11. The repair person <u>has not</u> arrived yet. _____

12. She <u>could not</u> come this morning. _____

13. I <u>cannot</u> call my aunt in Texas. _____

14. It <u>was not</u> always easy to talk to
someone far away. _____

15. A hundred years ago people <u>did not</u>
have telephones. _____

16. Alexander Graham Bell <u>had not</u>
invented them yet. _____

WRITE IT

Pretend there are no telephones. Write what it is like without
telephones. Use contractions in your sentences. Write on a
separate sheet of paper.

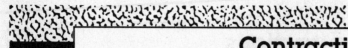

Contractions

Read the sentence pairs. Each pair includes a contraction. Underline the shortened forms of the verb and <u>not</u>.

1. The people are not happy.

   The people aren't happy.

2. They did not see the sun.

   They didn't see the sun.

 Some contractions are formed from a verb and <u>not</u>. An apostrophe (') shows where letters have been left out.

A. Circle the contraction in each sentence. Then write it in the blank.

EXAMPLE: The train (isn't) going to be late.   _____isn't_____

1. I don't hear a sound.   _____

2. It hasn't whistled yet.   _____

3. She wasn't very worried.   _____

4. I still can't see the smoke.   _____

5. We haven't waited too long.   _____

6. We weren't in a rush.   _____

B. Write the contraction for the words in ( ).

EXAMPLE: We _____weren't_____ prepared for rain. (were not)

7. The reporter _____ correct. (was not)

8. She _____ see the storm. (does not)

9. I _____ take my umbrella. (did not)

10. They _____ found their boots. (have not)

11. We _____ going out right now. (are not)

12. The rain _____ last too long. (should not)

Antonyms

A. In each sentence, write the antonym for the underlined word.

1. Zoey wants <u>more</u> corn, and Zack wants _____ .

2. The bedroom is <u>cool</u>, but the kitchen is _____ .

3. Tim wishes to <u>stay</u> at the zoo, but Flo wants to _____ .

4. Four puppies look <u>alike</u>, and one looks _____ .

5. You can <u>take</u> my puzzle if you _____ me your jump rope.

6. The hall closet is <u>neat</u>, but the bedroom closet is _____ .

7. Eva's hair is <u>short</u>, and Paula's hair is _____ .

8. She went to the airport <u>early</u>, but her plane was _____ .

9. It is <u>light</u> in the daytime and _____ at night.

10. The elevator was going <u>up</u>, but I wanted to go _____ .

B. Write the antonym for each word. Write one letter on each line. Use the circled letters to write the antonym of a "work night."

11. bottom   ___ ___ ◯ ___ ___

12. half   ___ ___ ___ ◯ ___

13. asleep   ___ ___ ◯ ___ ___

14. sad   ___ ___ ___ ___ ◯

15. up   ◯ ___ ___ ___

16. first   ___ ◯ ___ ___

17. no   ◯ ___ ___

___ ___ ___ ___ ___ ___ ___ ___

Antonyms

Antonyms are words that have opposite meanings. What antonyms do you think of for each pair?

_____   _____   _____   _____

A. Circle the two words in each sentence that are antonyms.

   EXAMPLE: Maine is (north) of Delaware, and Georgia is (south) of it.

   1. Dad tries to be early, but he usually is late.

   2. Fur is soft, and wood is hard.

   3. The city is very different from the country.

   4. A duck looks tiny next to a huge elephant.

   5. Was the spelling test difficult or easy?

   6. It is better to laugh than to cry.

B. Write the word in each row that means the opposite of the word in dark print.

EXAMPLE: **after**	soon	before	later	_before_
7. **brave**	afraid	strong	lovely	_____
8. **bright**	dull	sunny	smart	_____
9. **quick**	fast	speedy	slow	_____
10. **begin**	start	end	stay	_____
11. **exciting**	boring	interesting	lively	_____
12. **foolish**	silly	careless	wise	_____
13. **funny**	nice	sad	late	_____
14. **shiny**	hard	bumpy	dull	_____

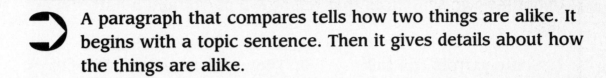

A Paragraph That Compares

A paragraph that compares tells how two things are alike. It begins with a topic sentence. Then it gives details about how the things are alike.

A. Read the topic sentence. Underline the two sentences that tell how the two things are alike.

1. Crayons and colored marking pens are alike in many ways.
   Both come in many colors.
   You can draw interesting pictures with both of them.
   They come with tops.

2. Records and tapes have some things in common.
   You use them only one time.
   You need a machine to play both of them.
   Both can tell stories.

3. In some ways board games and card games are alike.
   The players take turns.
   Each player gets seven cards.
   Each player follows the same directions.

B. Read the topic sentence. Then write a detail sentence that tells how the two things are alike.

4. In some ways basketball and football are alike.

   _____

5. Bicycles and roller skates are alike in some ways.

   _____

WRITE IT

Write a paragraph that compares two games or toys. Name the things you are comparing in the topic sentence. Then tell at least two ways the things are alike. Write on a separate sheet of paper.

A Paragraph That Compares

Underline two sentences that tell how a parrot and a butterfly are alike.

1. Some parrots can talk.   **3.** They both have beautiful colors.

2. They can both fly.   **4.** Butterflies are insects.

Read the topic sentence below. Finish the paragraph with the two detail sentences you underlined.

A butterfly and a parrot are alike in some ways. _____

_____

 A **paragraph that compares** tells how two things are alike. It begins with a topic sentence. Then it gives details about how the things are alike.

A. Circle the words that tell how each pair of things is alike.

EXAMPLE: a hat and a shoe ⟨things to wear⟩   things to read

1. a leaf and a peach   green things   things that grow on trees

2. a roof and an umbrella   things that keep you dry
   parts of a house

3. a dog and a cat   common pets   animals that purr

4. a table and a chair   things to sit on   things that have legs

B. Read each topic sentence. Then circle the two details that could be mentioned in the paragraph.
EXAMPLE: Lettuce and string beans are alike in some ways.
   ⟨are green⟩   ⟨are vegetables⟩   are leafy

5. Ducks and robins have some things in common.

   are birds   can swim   have feathers

6. In some ways pencils and pens are alike.

   use ink   are used for writing   are long and thin